JOHN BOOZMAN
ARKANSAS

UNITED STATES SENATOR
WASHINGTON, D.C. 20510

July 1, 2021

I love to better understand our history because it's interesting and we can learn a lot from our past. Arkansas is blessed to have so many areas of historical significance. The Natural State played a pivotal role in westward expansion so it is important to preserve and protect this history.

From 1858 through 1861, the Butterfield Overland Trail served as the connector between the East and the quickly growing West. It provided reliable mail service and transportation of goods and people to the western frontier. It was the first transcontinental stage coach service. About 337 miles of the trail are in Arkansas with four segments already listed on the National Register of Historic Places.

In 2007, as a member of the U.S. House of Representatives, I introduced the *Butterfield Overland Trail Study Act* to evaluate the historic Ox-Bow Route for potential addition to the National Trails System. The measure was signed into law in 2009. After thoroughly analyzing its historical relevance, the National Park Service agreed it met the requirements to be a National Historic Trail.

The designation will be a fitting recognition for its contributions to the growth and development of our country and the state of Arkansas. I will be working with my colleagues to ensure this trail is appropriately preserved as a National Historic Trail for future generations to visit and learn about the settlement of our country.

Few original stops on the Butterfield Overland Trail exist today. The Potts Inn Museum in Pope County is one of the best preserved that remains. Its history is important and should be recognized.

I wish the Potts Inn continued success in its mission to share its history with the world.

John Boozman

July 2021

With the snow deep on the ground in February  of this year, we began this journey of collecting photos and stories of history of the Potts family and early Pottsville.   Without the support and encouragement of so many along the way, it would not have been possible for this project to be completed.

Thanks to the many who provided photos and documents:  Mayor Randy Tankersley and the City of Pottsville, Superintendent Larry Dugger ,  Pottsville School District, David Duffield, Tom Teeter, Linda Reasoner, Ross Loeser, Tonya and David Oates (Charles Oates Collection) Bob Crossman, Melanie Oates Wheeler, David B. Oates, Sue Roberts, Beverly Keener, Ralph Wilcox with Arkansas Historic Preservation Program, Debbie Byrd and the Pope County Historical Foundation..

Information for the early churches was generously provided by: Rev. Howard Wheeler for the Associate Reformed Presbyterian Church, by Rev. Jim Huffman and David Duffield for the Baptist Church and Kenneth Taylor and Ray Tucker for the Pottsville Methodist Churches.

To Gerald (Gerry) Ahnert of Syracuse, New York:   Consultant and Expert on all things Butterfield.   Without your help, this would have been a lesser work.   Thank you for hours of counsel; and for the important photographs from the life of John Butterfield, his family and the Butterfield Overland Mail Company.   Gerry, The tour you gave us of upstate New York where Butterfield lived, and the trip to Forest Hills Cemetery in Utica to see his grave, brought us full circle.  We are in your debt.

Recognition to those who shared stories and gave assistance:  Dr. Stanley Teeter, Joe Grimes, Susie Kroencke, Nora Land, Dean Ferguson, Jim Bob Humphrey, Bobby Braily and Tom Wing.

To our computer guru, Jason Jacovelli—what would have we done without you!

The reviewers who read all of the material and ALWAYS made helpful suggestions and tremendous encouragement:  Garry Penman, Cathy Baker, Lynn  Wyman, Doris Barge Weatherford, and Susanne Wagner Motley.

The one person that we want to give extra thanks is Kenneth Taylor. Throughout this project he has continued to bring us photos, told many stories of his childhood in Pottsville and spent time showing us the places and history of Pottsville.  Driving the area with him identifying locations gave us an understanding of the town from the time of his childhood.  Kenneth is 93 years young and has a wonderfully sharp mind.  He called us "you girls" and after every story, he would say, "Now you know that has been a day or two ago!"  Thanks Kenneth!  It has been a real adventure.

To our families:  Dave Bowers and children Killian and Mel, and Allan Motley.  Thank you for your support and patience over these months.  Most of the photos identified as Author's collection were taken by Allan Motley and we appreciate so much the beautiful photographs.   Thank you!

"The Potts Family and Early Pottsville" has been a true JOY for both of us.

**Kara Bowers**                                        **Margaret Motley**

"I live in the Arkansas Territory, four hundred miles from any of my connections....I have been living here near two years and raise more corn and wheat than we consume but live on a public road where I can sell all the surplus...My sister, I must tell you that I see more pleasure and happiness now than I ever did in my life living with a fine and agreeable woman...I do not think I should tell you a lie if I should say that two hundred families moved by us last fall and winter principally from Kentucky and Tennessee, some, few from Missouri...I write in a hurry but do not fail to answer this as soon as you get it and direct to me Pope County, Galley Creek, Arkansas Territory."
Kirkbride Potts to his sister Ann Potts (Bordentown, NJ) on July 1, 1830.

Kirkbride Potts set down roots near Galley or Galla Creek before Pope County was organized. Kirkbride chose an area with woods, tall grasses, and canebrakes on the first bench of Crow Mountain to homestead. There he built a two story log cabin and began raising his family. From the home's position on the old military road, the Potts sold excess goods to families heading west and offered clean and comfortable accommodations to those seeking rest. It was from this home Kirkbride served as an Indian agent; and later made his impact heading west during the California gold rush, seeking a business opportunity beyond mining for gold....Cattle.

Potts wasn't the only one to see a future in the Arkansas River Valley. The River Valley's verdant landscape had attracted Methodist pioneers who settled to the west of Galley Creek closer to present day Russellville. At the same time wagon trains of Presbyterian pioneers leaving the Carolinas for this new land. By the 1850's, the Presbyterians had established a church, graveyard, and school a few miles from the Potts family in an area they called Pisgah. The area was growing.

Construction of the new Potts' home, known as Potts Station or Potts Inn, was finished in 1858, just in time to welcome the first Butterfield Overland Mail Stagecoach. Operating as the Overland Mail Company, the stagecoach service provided a vital link between the east and west. The Overland Mail Company operated on a regular twice per week schedule and traveled twenty four hours a day, seven days a week.  Stops were made at regular intervals to change horse or mule teams, and at places like Potts Station where meals and lodging were also offered.  Within three short years, the mail route would be pushed north as the rumblings of war spread across the country.

Small communities found themselves divided over questions of slavery and secession from the Union.  Most able-bodied men in Pope County volunteered for service and believed the war would be short lived.  The women, children, and older men left behind had to deal with bushwhackers and jayhawkers who wished to take advantage.

"Ruffians called at the Sinclair home seeking gold.  They refused to believe there was no more gold hidden by the Sinclairs.  The bandits heated a fire shovel red hot and threatened to burn the soles of old Gregory Sinclair's feet.  When Nancy McElwee Oates refused to tell where their gold was they carried out their threat."
William Oates Ragsdale, "They Sought a Land" (Fayetteville: University Press, 1997), 86.

Whether or not communities survived depended very much on the strength and resourcefulness of women and neighbors who stuck together.  The end of the war did not bring peace to Pope County.  Bitterness and Anger led to politically motivated assassinations against the Reconstruction Government in Pope County.  This unrest continued in the River Valley and other areas of Arkansas until Elisha Baxter was elected governor.

The intercontinental railroad attributed to the slow but steady economic recovery of the region  after the war.  By 1873, the railroad had been completed through Pope County.  Having a depot in the county was guaranteed to increase travel and community development.  Travel and the transportation of goods no longer relied on the river.  Stores and businesses opened and flourished..  The first large brick building was completed in 1887 and housed a general merchandise store.   Slowly, people began moving closer to Potts Station and over time, the churches followed.

Pamelia Potts passed away in August of 1878.  Only fifteen months later, in November of 1879, Kirkbride followed.  In 1897,

James Potts humbly asked that the town be named Pottsville in honor of his beloved and respected father.  Thus Pottsville was born.  The town was incorporated on May 7, 1897.

Pottsville grew.  The town center was located between the Potts Inn and the train depot.  Highway 64 ran right through it all.  The town had a post office, a large cotton gin, numerous stores, blacksmiths and by 1913, a bank.

"Verbal agreements existed between the various retailers that they would not sell certain products.  The service station did not sell tobacco products and the grocery stores did not sell motor oil.  The drug store alone had a freezer and was the only source for ice cream products in town."
James (Pete) Blake interview August 22, 2000.

Low prices on agricultural products after World War I and subsequent droughts and floods were already taking a toll on the agricultural economy of Pottsville and the surrounding areas in the 1920s, before the stock market crashed in 1929.  In spite of the economic collapse, many of Pottsville's businesses managed stay open.

"My Dad was a foreman for the WPA in this area.  He got the rock out of Galla Creek for the building of the high school gym.  That was probably 1936.."
Kenneth Taylor interview June 11, 2020.

Times were hard during the great depression; many people were unable to find employment.  The Public Works Administration (PWA) and Works Progress/Projects Administration (WPA), created as part of the New Deal, helped put people to work and made improvements throughout the area possible.  The WPA hired skilled and unskilled workers directly and paid them to construct buildings, improve/pave roads, and build small bridges.

Life changed again for Pottsville in December 1941.  Pearl Harbor was attacked, and America was thrust into another war.  Many citizens of Pottsville answered the call and joined the war effort.  Between those who left for military service and those who left to work in the factories, Pottsville was changing.

Residents of "Dog Alley" now live on Cedar Street.   The iconic iron bridge over Galla Creek has been replaced with a modern one.  The railway still runs through Pottsville.  The depot is gone, and the train no longer stops.  Highway 64 doesn't run through the downtown anymore, and many businesses have followed its relocation north of town.  Yet, the sense of community survives.

Potts Inn was listed on the National Historic Register in 1970.  Thanks in large part to Marge Crabaugh, Pope County purchased the Inn from the Potts family.  Working with the county officials and community members, a foundation was formed to oversee the preservation and upkeep of the Inn.

Today, the Potts Inn continues to welcome visitors to the area.  It's proudly featured on the local police department's badges and displayed in city hall.  And will continue the tradition of proudly welcoming visitors to Pottsville and the Potts Inn.

# The Potts Family

John Kirkbride Potts was born in Pennsylvania on November 23, 1803. He and his family spent some time in New Jersey before heading west. While traveling, the Potts became acquainted with the Robert Logan family and both families traveled together to Arkansas. On Christmas Day, 1828, Kirkbride began construction on a two story log home. Once finished, he married Robert Logan's daughter, Pamelia.

They lived in this home for almost thirty years. They raised a large family of eleven children, nine surviving until adulthood. Kirkbride and Pamelia were active and well respected citizens; active in service to the community. During the years preceding the Civil War, their home was a major stopping point for those traveling to and from the frontier. Attorney Albert Pike and other circuit riding lawyers and political leaders all stayed at the home known for its good food and hospitality. Newspaper articles told of the stops at the Potts' home by members of the Cherokee, Choctaw, Seminole and Creek tribes. Reports also related the resolution of difficult situations by Kirkbride.

When the Gold Rush began in 1849, Kirkbride joined those headed west looking for opportunity. He saw such an opportunity in feeding the miners. Instead of mining for gold, he returned home and organized large cattle drives to supply meat to the hungry forty-niners. The profits were used to construct the Potts Inn. During the early 1850's construction was begun on a new home. The new home was located on a small hill overlooking Galla Creek about a mile south of the first home.

The Potts Inn served as the family's home, an Inn, a stagecoach stop, a post office, and place for community gatherings. After Pamelia and Kirkbride passed, their son, James and his wife Ada moved in and began raising their own family in the home.

With this transition, while the Inn still hosted traveling salesmen, traveling ministers and other visitors regularly, James brought a new vision to Pottsville. Educated as a surveyor, elected a county clerk, employed in the banking industry....James continued to help Pottsville adjust to the changing times.  He was described by those who knew him as a real "southern gentleman and kind to everyone who crossed his path".  He and Ada were known to entertain often and enjoyed sumptuous dinners with friends  They continued the legacy of his father..

Their daughter, Mary Bradford Potts, never married and remained living with her parents until they passed.  James, had become blind in the decade before he died in 1932, and she and her mother cared for him.  Ada died in 1935.

This daughter of James and Ada Potts, Mary, was the last of the generations of the family to live in the house.  She and her brother's widow, Faye, lived there until the county bought the Potts Inn in 1970.

Kirkbride Potts was an early pioneer in the Arkansas Territory in the 1820s.  Originally, he settled south of the Arkansas River in what is now Logan County.  After an 1828 treaty with the western band of the Cherokee tribe, the government allowed Kirkbride to purchase 160 acres of land for 25 cents per acre in the area known as Galla or Galley, now known as Pottsville. *Courtesy of Pope County Historical Foundation.*

Early Map (May, 1839) of the Pottsville area where the Military Road crossed Galla Creek. Kirkbride had land holdings in sections 17, 18, 19, and 20. *Courtesy of the Pope County Historical Foundation.*

*Courtesy of Ralph Wilcox, Arkansas Historic Preservation*

The first Potts' home was built in 1828.  The two story log cabin was located close to both Galla Creek and the Military Road. Known for its cleanliness, hospitality, and good food, many travelers planned their trips to spend the night there.  No known photos of the house exist, but the hand dug well at their home place on the first bench of Crow Mountain is shown.  The family lived at this location until 1858.  *Author's collection.*

<u>Portions of Letters from Kirkbride to his sister Ann in New Jersey</u>
<u>About the Mail:</u>

July 1, 1830- Your letter was mailed at St. Louis May 24 and you see it was better that one month until I received it, but I have got letters from St. Louis in 14 days and now I intend this to go a more direct course.

Nov 3, 1848- Your kind letter bearing date the 13th September came to hand a few days ago being better than a month on the way. We were much pleased to hear from you as I had been looking for a letter for some time.

Oct 2, 1849- I was much pleased to get a letter from you for I declare I had almost despaired of your ever writing again.

<u>Life and Society:</u>

July 1, 1830- I have always remarked that a man who leads a sober, honest, and industrious life will never fail to have friends in any country.

Sept 25, 1846- We have a very good society here preaching every Sabbath and often through the week, so I do not think our country could be objected to on that account and it is setting up pretty fast with a very industrious pious people.

Sarah, Kirkbride's oldest daughter, wrote to Ann Potts in New Jersey

Jan 23, 1849- If you could be here once and become acquainted with all of our  good neighbors and see the sociability, hospitality, charity, liberality, sympathy, and independence that reign throughout our state all of which are emblematic of it.

<u>Plans for a Home:</u>

Nov 3, 1848- Could you get the draft of a convenient farm house and send it to me.  I told you I had an idea of building and I am at a loss for a good and convenient plan to build upon.  We have had a great deal of company since we got home and being in such a public place we have not house room enough.  Last night, we had 13 members with us going to the Legislature and we have someone almost every night.

Numerous letters have been preserved between the Potts family. Small portions of the letters from both Kirkbride and his oldest daughter, Sarah, illustrate the importance of mail and community in early Arkansas. *Courtesy of the PCHF.*

*Are you sure my strength is equal*
*To the tasks I daily do*
*That I never need assistance*
*Or encouragement from you?*

*Are you sure I don't miss it*
*The old love light in your eye?*
*The tender words once spoken*
*In the days long, long gone by?*

*Are you sure I'm never lonely*
*When you're absent from my side*
*Ah! The heart is crying always*
*For companionship denied*

*Are you sure you understand me*
*Or appreciate my worth?*
*Must you wait to be awakened*
*When no longer I'm on earth?*

*Original poem by Pamelia Potts*
*Pottsville, Arkansas*

Travel, like mail, was slow and often times treacherous. This poignant poem written by Pamelia Potts expresses the loneliness she felt for her husband, Kirkbride, during his three trips to the California gold fields. *Courtesy of the Pope County Historical Foundation.*

Located about one mile south of their first home on a small hill overlooking Galla Creek, the home was built in the Greek Revival Architectural style similar to the fine homes Kirkbride was familiar with in Pennsylvania.  The home was completed in 1858. *Courtesy of the Pope County Historical Foundation.*

This magnificent structure would be the home to three generations of the Potts family until was purchased by the Pope County Historical Foundation in 1970.  It currently serves as Pope County's only museum. *Author's collection.*

Potts family well water was known for its fine quality and used by many of the area residents. Local ladies frequently used this well's water for both making tea and washing their hair. Kirkbride's great-grandson once wrote that in all of his travels, he never tasted water as sweet as this. *Author's collection.*

Beside the well, a small water box is connected to the well house. Water was poured into the box and flowed into a cooling vat inside. Items such as milk and butter would be placed inside the water vat to stay cool. Once the water became warm, a plug would be pulled to drain it and more cool water from the well would be added. The well-water box design served as an early refrigeration system and was very important for the family. *Author's collection*

When the family was ready to move from the original location, Pamelia requested that the logs from the old home be used for the smokehouse. She said there was so much love in the first home she wanted to bring a reminder of it to the new place. The smokehouse was used to cure and store smoked meats enjoyed by both the family and their numerous guests. *Author's collection.*

Family wash day was a huge job with water brought to a boil in a large pot outdoors and then clothes hung on a clothes line to dry. *Authors collection.*

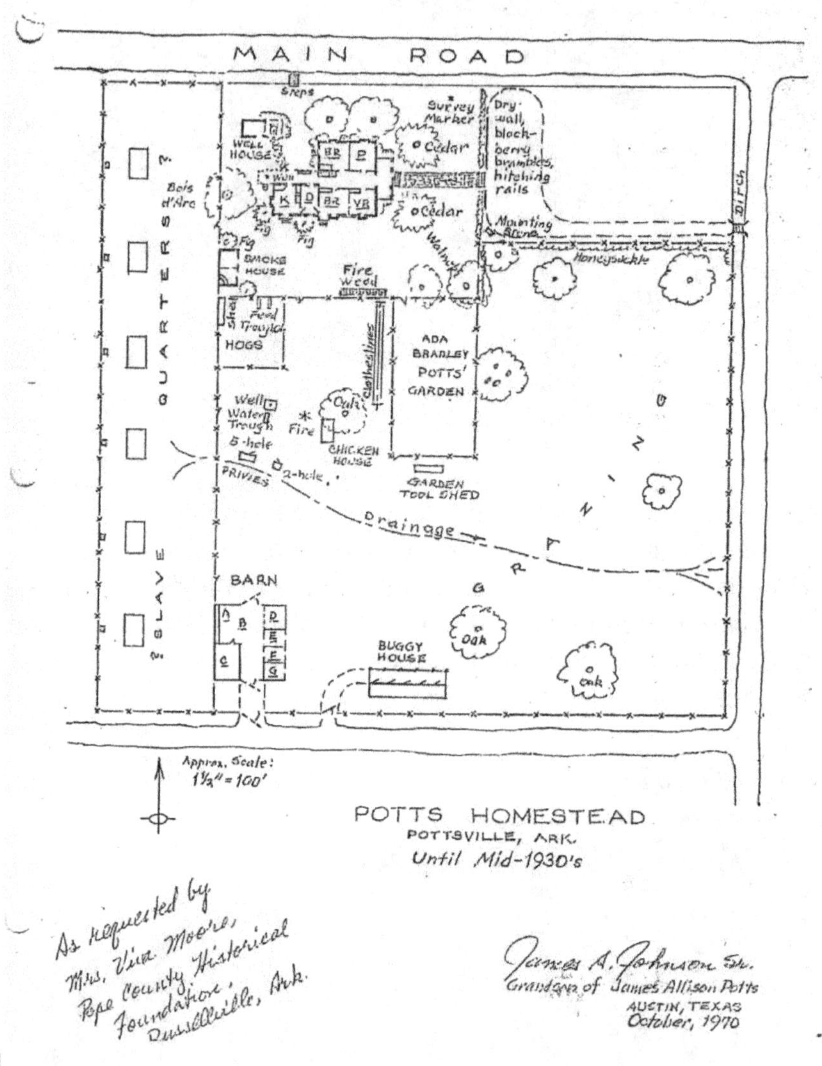


In October 1970, James Allison Johnson constructed a map of the Potts Inn property as he remembered it in the 1920s. A great-grandson of Kirkbride and Pamelia, James spent time as child with his grandparents, James and Ada Potts at the Inn. *Courtesy of the Pope County Historical Foundation.*

Potts Inn features a wide "dogtrot" hallway. The large "breezeway" through the center of the house was designed to allow air flow and keep the occupants of the home cool during the hot and humid Arkansas summers. *Author's collection.*

As the name suggests, the Gentlemen's Parlor was used by men to discuss important topics of the era like politics, crop prices, and weather. Other family pieces include the writing desk and the six matching pressed wood straight chairs (1910). *Author's collection.*

The Gentlemen's Parlor contains a patent or carpet rocker that came to Arkansas from Pennsylvania with the Potts family.

Positioned against the west wall is an unusual desk. It offers all the standard needs of a desk but also includes a storage area for a rifle. *Author's collection.*

Ladies' Parlor, located to the right of the front door, was the formal room used for special events and entertaining.  Daughters of the Potts family were married in front of the fireplace.  Large Christmas celebrations and community events have been held and recorded throughout the years.  The chandelier is a very early oil lamp, and the full square grand piano was donated by the family of Reese Hogins, a Pope County Sheriff who served in the 1880s and was later elected Mayor of Russellville.  *Author's collection.*

The painting of Palm Sunday was done by a German prisoner of war (POW) in Chicot County, Arkansas during World War II.  Mary Johnson Hall Hawkins (5-12-1912--6-4-2014), a great-granddaughter of Kirkbride and Pamelia Potts, and her family lived in Chicot County close to the Camp Dermott POW camp.  Mary oversaw the sugar rationing program for the county.  She used sugar from her own allotment to make treats for the prisoners.  When she discovered an artist in the group, she procured the necessary items for him to do a painting for her.

Mary was a huge supporter of preserving the Potts home and worked tirelessly with Marge Crabaugh to achieve that goal.  In later years, she donated the painting to the Potts Inn Museum where it is on display in the Ladies Parlor. *Author's collection.*

A large dining room was needed to accommodate the numerous family members, guests, and travelers passing through.  The family used Alfred Meakin china in the Lynn pattern.  The corner cupboards of cherry and walnut wood (1865-1870) were used for china and linen storage.  In the corner sits a pie safe with screening on the sides.  It was used to store pies, cakes, biscuits, and jellies. *Photos Author's collection.*

The decorative bowl was a gift given by Kirkbride and Pamelia's grandson G L to his store customers in Carden Bottoms, Yell County.   Bowl was donated to the museum by Joe Grimes in 2021.

One of the large bedrooms was located downstairs.  This room was used by both Kirkbride and his wife Pamelia and later by James and his wife Ada.  The white metal wash stand used to hold a washbowl, pitcher, towels, and chamber pot belonged to Kirkbride Potts, and the bed in the room was owned by James and Ada Potts.  *Author's collection.*

Treadle sewing machine used by the Potts Family.  Donated to the Inn by Barbie James, great, great granddaughter of Kirkbride and Pamelia.  *Author's collection.*

Known as a flyaway staircase, it would have been built by an expert craftsman. The straight section of the handrail is comprised of a single piece of wood without any seams. According to the children in the family, it was perfect for sliding down. After more than a century of use, the steps and balustrade remain solid. *Author's collection.*

Most of the materials used in constructing Potts Inn were gathered from the local area. Clay from nearby Galla Creek was used in these brick molds to make all the bricks used in the chimneys and the well house. *Author's collection.*

Side saddle belonging to Mary Hall, granddaughter of James and Ada Potts. *Author's collection.*

Four large bedrooms comprise the upstairs.  Each room would be furnished with four beds, washbowls, and chamber pots.  The four-bed arrangement allowed the Inn to accommodate up to thirty two guests at a time, meaning that travelers would share rooms and possibly beds depending on the number of guests.  *Author's collection.*

Known as a fainting couch, this piece is on display at the Potts Inn Museum.  *Author's collection.*

In the northwest bedroom upstairs is contains the baby carriage Pamelia used for all her children. The large wicker buggy could hold both an infant and toddler when necessary.  A cradle served as the baby's bed to keep them close, and later as a bed for the children's dolls. *Author's collection.*

A spinning wheel was an important part of any pioneer household. This spinning wheel, known as a great wheel, was used to spin short fibers such as cotton and wool into thread or yarn.  The popping sound that a yarn or spinner's weasel makes when full may have given the song lyric in, "Pop Goes the Weasel."  *A penny for a spool of thread, another for a needle, that's the way the money goes, Pop! Goes the weasel!  Author's collection.*

Every bedroom contained a place to wash up.  A pitcher of water and a bowl was provided along with clean towels.  *Author's collection.*

Located on the south wall of the northeast bedroom is a section of the wall that has been opened to illustrate how the plaster walls were constructed.  The thin flat strips of wood, called laths, form the foundation for the plaster.  The plaster was usually made using powered lime, sand, and some sort of fiber.  Horse hair was the fiber used in Potts Inn plaster.  The small gaps between the laths allow the plaster to form a bond with laths. Each wall received at least three layers of plaster and provided some insulation, sound dampening, and fire resistance. *Author's collection.*

The large attic offers a look at the timber frame construction.  Logs
were hewn by hand to create the flat faces and edges of the beams.
Wooden pegs and notches were used hold the beams together.
Generally, this type of construction did not require nails.  The
picture below offers a view of the foundation.  *Author's collection.*

*Courtesy of Ralph Wilcox, Arkansas Historic Preservation
Program.*

A second floor balcony offered views of the surrounding area and town.  During the summer's heat and humidity, the family would often pull a mattress out on to the balcony to sleep at night.

Mary Hall remembers sleeping on the front balcony with her grandmother when two robbers blew the safe at the Falls-Sinclair across the street.  When the sheriff from Russellville and Mr. Falls came the next day to ask what we knew, I said, " I can tell you.  They went toward the depot and they were in a big hurry"  That must have been important information, for the robbers were caught that evening in Morrilton, just twenty miles away.

*Author's collection.*

Before the days of indoor plumbing, using the bathroom meant a trip outside, usually a short distance from the home. At night; however, going outside could mean contending with wet or cold weather, so other options such as a chamber pot were employed.  *Author's collection.*

Over the years, the outhouse would have changed as the family's needs changed.  It would have been located a short distance from the house in the barn area.  In the busy days of the stagecoach, it was reported to be a six holer, then four and then a two holer.

Mary Hall remembers that the outhouse was always kept clean and smelling good.  The rule was to close the door when in use, and leave it open for the next person.

Early homes did not have a kitchen as part of the main structure. Kitchens and cooking required an open flame which produced heat and odors. If a fire occurred, having separate buildings protected the main house and the occupants inside. The wide assortment of cooking utensils and cast iron cookware were needed to prepare and cook for the large Potts family and the travelers and guests who frequently stopped in. *Author's collection.*

Knives displayed in the Potts family kitchen have been appraised by world-renown Russellville knife expert Jimmy Lile.  Most of the knives were made by early settlers; however, two of the knives were made by Native American groups in the area.  The Native American knives have a rounded handle without pins.  *Author's collection.*

Without the ease of indoor plumbing, bathing took much more planning and work.  Water had to be drawn from the well and heated over a fire.  It was then poured in the tub which sat nearby usually inside the kitchen.  The bucket-by-bucket process was repeated until the tub was full.  Afterwards, each person took a turn bathing. The last person to bathe had the job of emptying the bath water when finished.  *Author's collection.*

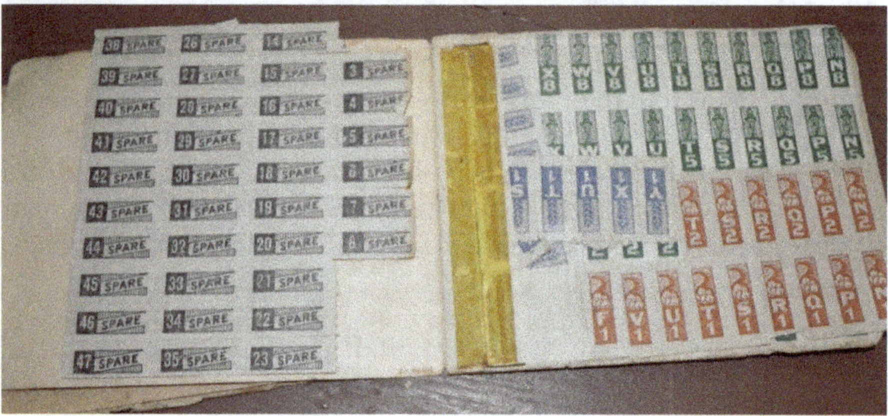

Shown in the museum kitchen are war ration stamps and cards that would have been used during World War II. Materials and items needed for the war effort were in short supply and rationing was a way to ensure each person received their fair share. According to an article by George Jones, Coach and Teacher at Pottsville Schools, he remembers, it was in 1943 during World War II that the Pottsville School District dismissed school for the day in order for teachers to register people for their rationing stamps. Sugar was one of the first commodities rationed, but by the end of the war, almost every product except eggs and dairy were limited. *Author's collection.*

Potts Inn has been a popular site for the community since it was completed.  Whether depicted with shutters on the windows or a split rail fence in the front, Potts Inn has been a popular backdrop for weddings and class photos.  Recently,  a photo of Potts Inn has been added to the badges of the local police department. *Author's collection.*

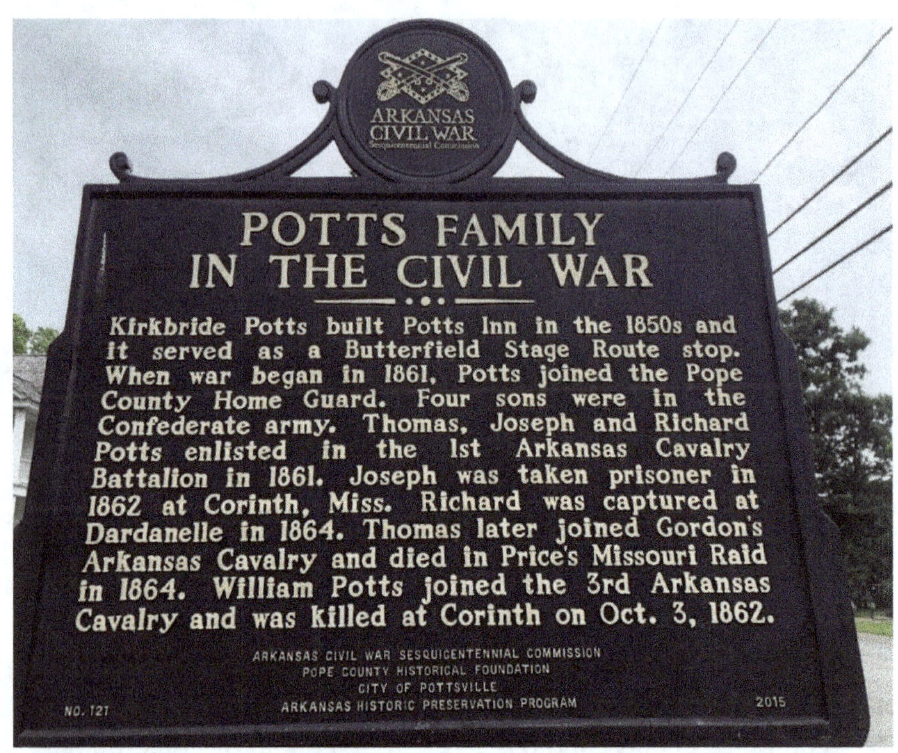



The Potts family suffered along with the entire nation during the Civil War (1861-1865).  Although the Inn itself survived the war intact, the family paid a steep price.  According to the Arkansas Gazette on January 30, 1866---"Kirkbride Potts of Potts Tavern sent five of his sons to the Confederate Army; two never came back and details of their deaths are unknown to this day." *Author's collection.*

The Confederate dollar, first issued in April 1861, was the primary means by which the Confederacy planned to finance the civil war against the United States of America. The Confederate dollar was not backed by any tangible asset, such as gold, making it a promissory note or bill of credit. Repayment of notes was to have occurred six months after the successful conclusion of the war.

When the Confederates surrendered in 1865, these bills became practically useless. When Ross Loeser was a boy in the 1950's visiting the Potts relatives, they gave him these bills as a keepsake. *Courtesy of Ross Loeser, great, great grandson of Kirkbride Potts.*

AMERICAN FIRE AND CASUALTY COMPANY

CONSERVATIVE RATES - - PREFERRED RISKS ONLY

EXCHANGE BUILDING
ORLANDO, *Florida*

A STOCK COMPANY

ADDRESS REPLY TO

ERNEST D. ALLMON
109 BOULDER
P. O. BOX 451
TELEPHONE 768
RUSSELLVILLE, ARKANSAS

Knoweth all Men by these presents, that Kirkbride Potts and Pamela A. Potts
for and in consideration of one dollar to them in hand paid, and in consideration
of the benefits to accrue to them and their heirs from the building of the Little
Rock and Fort Smith Railroad, they do hereby grant bargain, and quit claim into the
Little Rock and Fort Smith Railroad Company a right of way to the said Compoany ,
being two hundred feet, the middle thereof to be the track of said road, throuth
the following lands lying in Pope County, Arkansas to wit: SW¼ Sec tion 1 of SW ¼
SE ¼ ~~SxxkimxxixmfxSRxx~~ Section 1 of and N½ NE¼ Section 20 all in T of N R lq W.
To have and to hold the same ƚo said Railroad Co pany forever,  Withess our hands
and seals on this 24th day of November, 1869.

Witness:                                    Kirkbride Potts (Seal)
James A. Martin                             P. A. Potts    (Seal)
J. C. Martin

In 1869 Kirkbride and Pamelia Potts deeded a right away through their land to the Little Rock and Fort Smith Railroad Company.

 Family members say there was always a positive relationship between the Potts family and the railroad. *Courtesy of the Pope County Historical Foundation.*

In Memoriam of Pamelia Logan Potts

The Democrat, August 22, 1878

"The public press from time to time, as the great and the good of this world are taken away to their eternal rest, place upon record their good deeds and pay appropriate tribute to their memories.  Some have written their deeds high upon the scroll of fame, the lives of many have been acted out so conspicuously in the presence of their fellowmen that the mere announcement of their deaths, of itself, calls to mind the good works they have performed;  and causes the panorama of a well spent life to pass before the mind's eye.  There are others, whose lives have been spent in the quiet, unobtrusive shades of private life, whose deeds though not emblazoned before the public, were of the kind which live after them in pious and beneficial results.  These thoughts are suggested by sad intelligence that the wife of one of the old Arkansas pioneers, Kirkbride Potts of Pope County, departed this life at her home, August 5, 1878 in the 68th year of her age.  Mrs. Potts' maiden name was Pamelia A. Logan, and she was born in Wayne County, Missouri, January 13th, 1811.

She was the daughter of Robert A. Logan, who moved from Kentucky to Missouri Territory in the year 1803, and held land under the Spanish Government.  From there, in 1823, he removed to the then Territory of Arkansas, and settled near Morrison' Bluff. This settlement was then known as Logan's Bottom, and in what is now the county of Logan.  Under an exchange of lands with the Cherokees which occurred in 1828, the Logan family settled at Galla Creek, where on the 10th day of February 1829, the daughter Pamelia, became Mrs. Kirkbride Potts.  In the immediate vicinity, for almost the full period of half a century, this good woman indeed a help-meet for the thrifty, industrious husband of her choice, and here as a result of such a life, did they reside in their old age, in a home which was the picture of thrift and comfort, while it was in the very truth the abode of hospitality.  Happy the traveler in days antedating  the Fort Smith Railroad, when in the course of his weary journey he found himself comfortably housed at "Potts", which was the most famous stage stand on the route.

Mrs. Potts came up to the full measure of a "farmer's wife" and much of the success of her husband is due to her active and wise domestic management.  The offspring from this marriage was 9 children, 7 boys and 2 girls.  Six of these survive their mother, and, with the exception of the eldest now residing in California, they all live in Pope or adjoining counties and are among the best and most highly esteemed citizens.  The quiet, but systemic and effective relief extended by Mrs. Potts to her poor neighbors, the acts of charity which mingled each day with the thrifty management of her household affairs, will cause her loss to be keenly felt and sincerely mourned by all who were ever so fortunate as to come within the circle of her kindly hospitality or kindlier benevolence.

May the father of all mercies console and comfort her bereaved family, and especially may he lead the venerable man who now walks solitary and alone in the shadow of a deep sorrow."

Death of Kirkbride Potts

Galley Creek, Pope Co. Ark.
Nov 25th, 1879

Editor Democrat--"Ever and anon the visitations of Providence
surround us with pain and sorrow, by calling from time to eternity,
some noble, generous and honored friend.

Last night the 24th inst. at 9 p.m.at his residence on Galley Creek
Pope Co., Ark, Mr. Kirkbride Potts departed this life after many
months of long and painful suffering from dyspepsia in its most
aggrandized form.  He had been a resident at the place of his decease

for over half a century, a period of fifty-one years.  He was born in
Pennsylvania on the 23d on Nov. 1803, and lived one day over the
76th anniversary of his birth which epoch he had expressed while
sick a desire to reach and attain, and did live to witness before he
died.  He lived on the Delaware river in New Jersey until nearly
grown when he moved to Missouri, from there he emigrated to and
temporarily settled in Logan's Bottom, now a part of Logan County,
Ark., at that time occupied by the Cherokee Indians, from there he
went to Sallisaw river, when by the treaty with the Cherokee nation
known as Lovely Purchase he was reduced to retrace his steps and
purchased the claim of a Cherokee Indian and located in company
with Robert A. and William Logan on Galla Creek on the 25th of
December 1828 where he has continually resided until his death.
On the 10th of February 1829 he was married to Miss Pamelia
Logan (the daughter of Robert A. Logan).  Mrs. Potts preceded him
to the grave on the 5th day of Aug. 1878 which affliction preyed
greatly upon his mind, happiness and health and had much to do
with hastening his departure.  He passed away without a struggle or
a long drawn breath, so gently that his exit resembled more that of
peaceful slumber than launching into the cold and icy arms of death.
No couple within my knowledge ever had greater cause to feel
thankful to Providence, than Mr. and Mrs. Potts, having lived
together to good old age, esteemed and well revered by all who
knew them, with a sufficiency of all the goods, and comforts of life,
blessed with a family of four sons and two daughters yet living,
respectable and valuable acquisitions and ornaments to any society
and community, and who were constant and incessant in their
attentions and devotions to them while they lived, and surrounding
their bedside during the last and trying moments of life,
administering comfort and endeavoring to soothe and make soft
their dying pillows.
Mrs. Sarah Carey his eldest daughter, of Colusa, California being
telegraphed for, reached her father's bedside on Friday the 14th
instant and with her only sister and her much loved brothers with
their wives hovered around his departing spirit with that deep and
devoted affection and love so richly deserved and merited by one of
the purest, best and honored parents, the kind neighbor, the
esteemed citizen, and beyond question or doubt, the poor man's most
invaluable friend.  Mr. Potts was widely known, universally loved

and esteemed, not only in Arkansas, but by many, very many in other states, for his domicile was an inviting and hospitable home to the weary traveler and pilgrim in a land which for a number of years was the lair of the wild beast of the forest, and the home of the Indian.  He will be sadly missed by a deeply grieved family of children, numerous relatives and the entire community.
The writer of this brief notice, having settled in Pope County one month after Mr. Potts came to it, knew him well and esteemed him greatly for his many valued traits of character and intricate worth, and having enjoyed his most intimate personal confidence and friendship for over a half a century, he can and does deeply sympathize with his family in their sad affliction and bereavement."

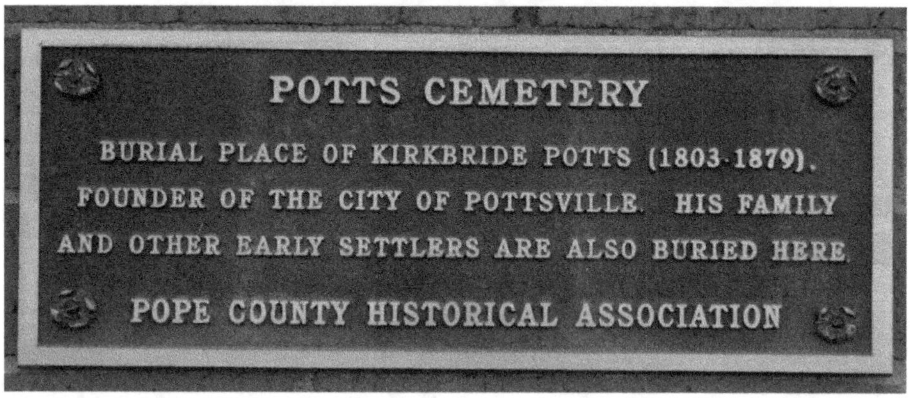


The Potts Family cemetery and historical marker. According to cemetery records, the earliest burial was March 1858. Kirkbride and Pamelia's infant twin daughters, (not named-one lived 1 day and the other 8 days). Also resting in the fenced Potts family plot Kirkbride and Pamelia, their son Charles who was 16 when he died September 12, 1868, sons, Joseph, Dr. John and wife Lucy Potts. Others buried in the cemetery: Pamelia's brother James Logan, and pioneer families Carpenters and Sleekers. These early settlers rest in this peaceful spot, across the railroad tracks from Potts Inn. *Author's collection.*

Ada Bradley Potts and James Allison Potts photographed in their home in Russellville shortly after they married in 1878. *Courtesy of the Pope County Historical Foundation.*

James and Ada Bradley Potts were the second generation to live in the Potts Inn.  Vestal is leaning against her father's arm, Ada is holding John, and Pamelia is kneeling on the ground.  Shown standing are (L to R):  Sarah, son Lorraine, LaVanche, Mary and Grace.

Later, Mary and her brother John's widow, Faye Potts would be the third generation to live in the house until it was sold to the Pope County Historical Foundation in 1970.  *Courtesy of the Pope County Historical Foundation.*

Adult children of James and Ada Potts with their mother:  L to R:
Ada Potts, Grace, Lorraine, Pamelia, Mary, Vestal

Grace Potts, granddaughter of Kirkbride and Pamelia Potts  in her wedding gown. *Courtesy of the Pope County Historical Foundation.*

Sarah Potts Johnson and her daughter, Mary Adelaide. The first of James and Ada Potts children to marry, Sarah and her husband Valter were married in the Potts family home on June 25, 1902. They were living in Porter, Oklahoma when Mary was born on May 31, 1912 just two years after Oklahoma became a state. Mary was the first great grandchild of the Kirkbride and Pamelia. *Courtesy of the Pope County Historical Foundation.*

Pamelia Beth Potts Ross, Kirkbride and Pamelia's granddaughter photographed in 1937. This beautiful dress would have been made by the Potts women who were known for their sewing skills. *Courtesy of Ross Loeser, grandson.*

The Potts family library is large.  Members of the family collected books on a variety of subjects including early education, religious writings, and foreign languages. Because James Potts was the County Surveyor, there are many books devoted to that subject. Education was taken very seriously, even the girls were sent to school and earned college degrees. *Author's collection.*

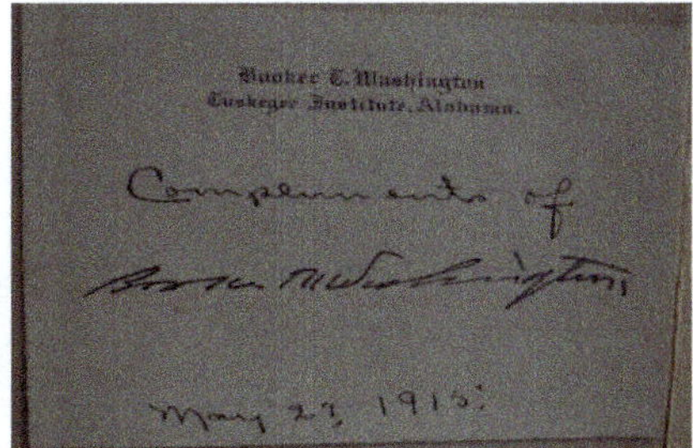

From the Library of James Potts; a SIGNED copy of "Working with the Hands" by famed African-American Booker T. Washington.  Published 1904, it was signed by Washington on one of his Tuskegee Institute bookplates which was then affixed.  He was an educator, author, and orator.  He was the founder and First President of Tuskegee Institute (Now Tuskegee University) Alabama.  He valued classroom education, but believed that education must be a balance of "hand, head and heart".

As a condition of admission, students served a full day of labor and received classroom study by night.  The students learned to become Entrepreneurs by literally building Tuskegee.    Students built the dormitories, made the bricks; became Agriculturalists and Culinary experts in growing what they ate.  They designed, built, and repaired farm tools.  They also made their own fashionable clothing.  Booker T. Washington stressed that "we teach our students to lift labor out of drudgery and to place it on the plane where it would become attractive, something to be sought after rather than dreaded and avoided."

Washington's success is measured by the business, religious, social and military leaders who trace their educational background back to Tuskegee Institute, and Booker T. Washington.
*Courtesy of the Pope County Historical Foundation.*

A  huge Bois d 'arc (bow wood) tree is located just west of the rear of the house.  Commonly known as an Osage Orange, early settlers planted Bois d 'arc trees together to form hedges that would grow together densely and protect fields and gardens from wandering animals.  Later after the introduction of barbwire, wood from the bois d 'arc tree was used for fence posts as it is a very hard wood that is rot resistant.  The exact age of this tree is unknown, but it's estimated to be very old. *Author's collection*

# Butterfield's Overland Mail Co.

John Butterfield was born in 1801 in Bern, New York.  By age 19 he was driving stagecoaches.  Butterfield grew up in the transportation industry, a conscientious young man, working several stagecoach lines in upstate New York.  This long, reputable and successful career in transportation placed him at the right moment in time to submit a bid to transport mail across the nation.  He was 56 years old when he founded what history remembers as The Butterfield Overland Mail Company..

In 1857 a U S Government bid was issued to carry the mail from St. Louis, MO and Memphis, TN, merging at Fort Smith, AR., then on to San Francisco, CA.  John Butterfield was awarded the six-year $600,000 annual contract with the requirement that the mail be delivered in 25 days or less.

Three and one half million dollars and a year of preparation was invested in the 2,860-mile trail.  Butterfield's son-in-law and three of his sons were involved in the planning.  Son Charles moved to Fayetteville, AR to oversee that stop.  On September 16, 1858 stages left at the same time from Madison, AR, and Tipton, MO, headed to Fort Smith.  The east-west stage through Arkansas arrived in Fort Smith fifteen minutes before the southbound stage. In Fort Smith, the passengers and mail were transferred from these stagecoaches to a stage wagon for the trip through the frontier.

The Butterfield Overland Mail stages traveled 24 hours a day, seven days a week, stopping only every 20 miles to change horses and grab quick meals.  The first run was completed in 23 days and 23 hours, one full day less than requirement of the contract.

The route through central Arkansas traveled from Memphis to Fort Smith mostly on the Old Military Road.  Potts Inn was a Home Station stagecoach stop.  Potts home was completed in 1858, just in time for the running of the first stage.  Kirkbride had been a Postal Agent for many years for the Galla (Galley) post office.  In the years that the stagecoach operated, it is estimated that over 300 stagecoach stops were made at Potts Inn.

The beginning of the Civil War in 1861 ended Butterfield's service on the Southern Overland Trail.  John Butterfield died in 1869 and is buried in Utica, NY.  He was a true American visionary.

John Butterfield, born on November 18, 1801 in upstate New York had a long career in the transportation industry. When the contract bid was opened in 1857, John's company was probably the most qualified, if not the only company prepared to oversee this massive job. Because of his years of experience and with his family and former employees' valuable assistance, he completed preparations in one year from the date the contract was awarded. On September 16, 1858, Butterfield's Overland Mail Company began their first successful run from Tipton, Missouri and Memphis, Tennessee to San Francisco. *Courtesy of the history of Oneida County, New York 1667-1878.*

Although John Butterfield purchased 34 stagecoaches and 66 stage (Celerity) wagons for the over three thousand mile trail, no examples of these stages remain today.  The company poured about three and a half million dollars into establishing the route. **[That is equivalent to $112,262,000 in 2021's purchasing power.]**  There were 1,800 horses and mules, and 3,000 tons of grain and hay delivered to the various stations along the route.  Drawings from the 1958 Centennial booklet by W. J. Lemke and Ted R. Worley show representations of the stagecoach traveling and stopping in front of a house.  *Courtesy of the Arkansas Centennial booklet.*

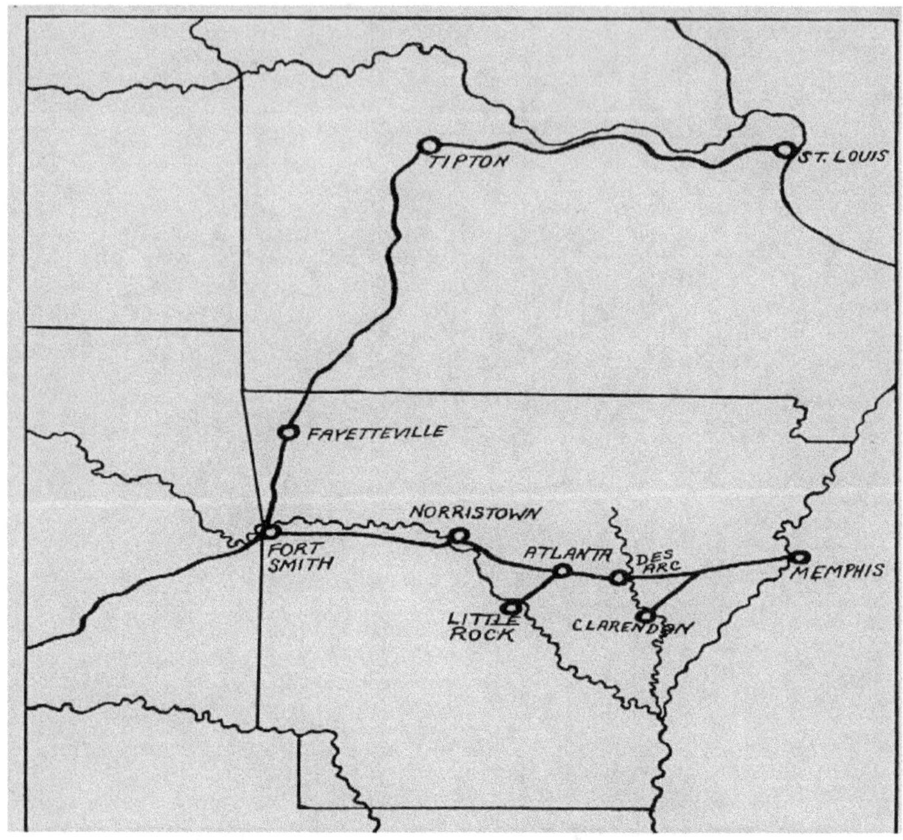



The map of Arkansas shows the Butterfield stagecoach line through the state.  One section came out of Missouri, through the Ozark Mountains and crossed the Arkansas River by ferry at Van Buren.  The east-west line was transporting mail from Memphis, along the north side of the Arkansas River, crossing by ferry at Norristown, across the river from Dardanelle.  A section to the Capitol City of Little Rock was added in January of 1859.  Although the Potts Inn is not shown on this map, it was the major Home Station between Memphis and Fort Smith.  *Courtesy of the Butterfield Overland Mail in Arkansas Centennial 1958 booklet.*

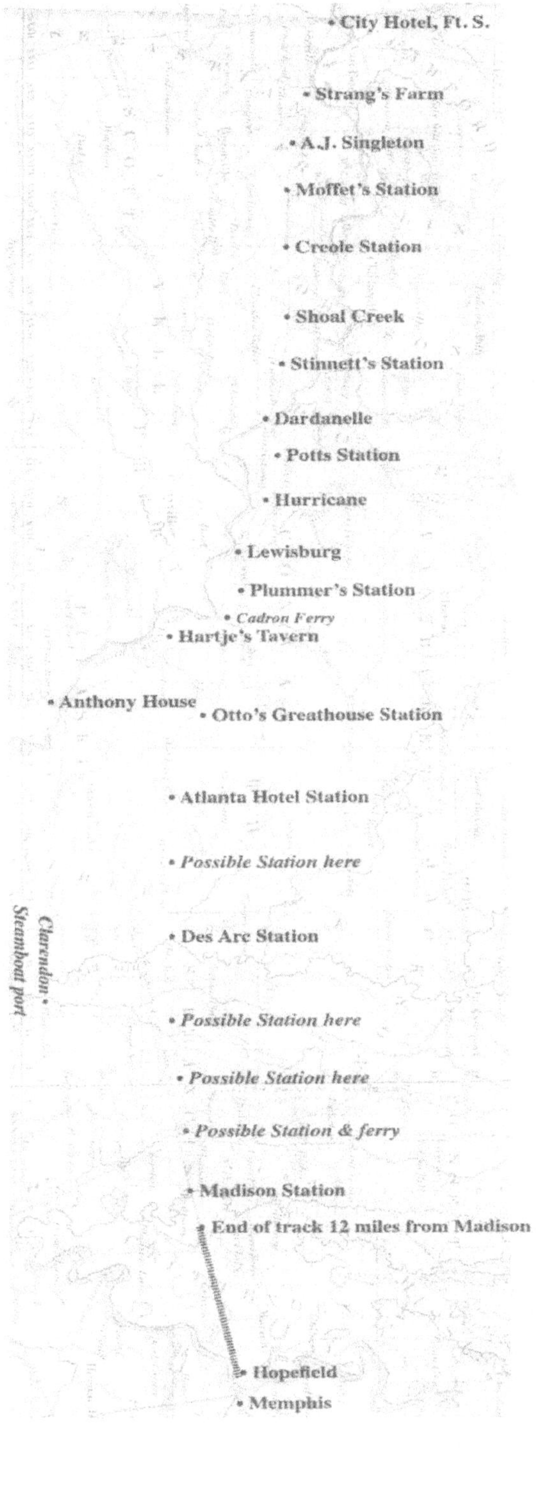

This map shows the known stagecoach stations which were located about 20 miles apart from Memphis to Fort Smith. Some stations were called swing stations, with only a couple of workers to change the tired horses for a fresh team. Others were Home Stations, such as the Potts Inn. At the home stations the drivers and passengers could get a quick twenty-minute meal and then back on the trail. The stage driver drove his section of approximately 60 miles and then he rested at that home station to return back on another day. *Courtesy of Bob Crossman.*

No. 1]  [Sep. 16th, 1858.

# OVERLAND MAIL COMPANY.

## THROUGH TIME SCHEDULE BETWEEN

### ST. LOUIS, MO., MEMPHIS, TENN. } & SAN FRANCISCO, CAL.

| GOING WEST. | | | | | | GOING EAST. | | | | | |
|---|---|---|---|---|---|---|---|---|---|---|---|
| LEAVE. | DAYS. | Hour. | Distance from Place to Place. | Time allowed. | Av'ge Miles per Hour. | LEAVE. | DAYS. | Hour. | Distance from Place to Place. | Time allowed. | Av'ge Miles per Hour. |
| | | | Miles. | No. Hours. | | | | | Miles. | No. Hours. | |
| St. Louis, Mo., & Memphis, Tenn. | Every Monday & Thursday. | 8.00 A.M | | | | San Francisco, Cal | Every Monday & Thursday. | 8.00 A.M | | | |
| P. R. R. Terminus, " | " Monday & Thursday. | 6.00 P.M | 160 | 10 | 16 | Firebaugh's Ferry, " | " Tuesday & Friday, | 11.00 A.M | 163 | 27 | 6 |
| Springfield, " | " Wednesday & Saturday | 7.45 A.M | 143 | 37¾ | 3¾ | Visalia, " | " Wednesday & Saturday, | 5.00 A.M | 82 | 18 | 4½ |
| Fayetteville, " | " Thursday & Sunday. | 10.15 A.M | 100 | 26¼ | 3¾ | Ft. Tejon, (via Los Angeles) | " Thursday & Sunday. | 9.00 A.M | 127 | 28 | 4½ |
| Fort Smith, Ark | " Friday & Monday, | 3.30 A.M | 65 | 17¼ | 3¾ | San Bernardino, " | " Friday & Monday, | 5.30 P.M | 150 | 32½ | 4½ |
| Sherman, Texas | " Sunday & Wednesday, | 12.30 A.M | 205 | 45 | 4½ | Fort Yuma, " | " Sunday & Wednesday. | 1.50 P.M | 200 | 44 | 4½ |
| Fort Belknap, " | " Monday & Thursday, | 9.00 A.M | 146½ | 32½ | 4½ | Gila River,* Arizona | " Monday & Thursday, | 7.30 P.M | 135 | 30 | 4½ |
| Fort Chadbourn, " | " Tuesday & Friday, | 3.15 P.M | 136 | 30½ | 4½ | Tucson, " | " Wednesday & Saturday | 3.00 A.M | 141 | 31¼ | 4½ |
| Pecos River, (Em Crossing) | " Thursday & Sunday, | 3.45 A.M | 165 | 36½ | 4½ | Soldier's Farewell, " | " Thursday & Sunday, | 8.00 P.M | 184½ | 41 | 4½ |
| El Paso, | " Saturday & Tuesday, | 11.00 A.M | 248½ | 55¼ | 4½ | El Paso, Tex. | " Saturday & Tuesday, | 5.30 A.M | 150 | 33½ | 4½ |
| Soldier's Farewell | " Sunday & Wednesday, | 8.30 P.M | 150 | 33½ | 4½ | Pecos River, (Em Crossing) | " Monday & Thursday | 12.45 P.M | 248½ | 55¼ | 4½ |
| Tucson, Arizona | " Tuesday & Friday, | 1.30 P.M | 184½ | 41 | 4½ | Fort Chadbourn, " | " Wednesday & Saturday | 1.15 A.M | 165 | 36½ | 4½ |
| Gila River,* " | " Wednesday & Saturday | 9.00 P.M | 141 | 31¼ | 4½ | Fort Belknap, " | " Thursday & Sunday, | 7.30 A.M | 136 | 30½ | 4½ |
| Fort Yuma, Cal. | " Friday & Monday, | 3.00 A.M | 135 | 30 | 4½ | Sherman, " | " Friday & Monday, | 4.00 P.M | 146½ | 32½ | 4½ |
| San Bernardino " | " Saturday & Tuesday, | 11.00 P.M | 200 | 44 | 4½ | Fort Smith, Ark | " Sunday & Wednesday, | 1.00 P.M | 205 | 45 | 4½ |
| Ft. Tejon, (via Los Angeles) | " Monday & Thursday, | 7.30 A.M | 150 | 32½ | 4½ | Fayetteville, Mo. | " Monday, & Thursday. | 6.15 A.M | 65 | 17¼ | 3¾ |
| Visalia, " | " Tuesday & Friday, | 11.30 A.M | 127 | 28 | 4½ | Springfield, " | " Tuesday & Friday, | 8.45 A.M | 100 | 26¼ | 3¾ |
| Firebaugh's Ferry, " | " Wednesday & Saturday | 5.30 A.M | 82 | 18 | 4½ | P. R. R. Terminus, " | " Wednesday & Saturday | 10.30 P.M | 143 | 37¾ | 3¾ |
| (Arrive) San Francisco, | " Thursday & Sunday. | 8.30 A.M | 163 | 27 | 6 | (Arrive) St. Louis, Mo., & Memphis, Tenn. | " Thursday & Sunday. | | 100 | 10 | 16 |

This Schedule may not be exact—Superintendents, Agents, Station-men, Conductors, Drivers and all employees are particularly directed to use every possible exertion to get the Stages through in quick time, even though they may be ahead of this time.

If they are behind this time, it will be necessary to urge the animals on to the highest speed that they can be driven without injury.

Remember that no allowance is made in the time for ferries, changing teams, &c. It is therefore necessary that each driver increase his speed over the average per hour enough to gain the necessary time for meals, changing teams, crossing ferries, &c.

Every person in the Company's employ will always bear in mind that each minute of time is of importance. If each driver on the route loses fifteen (15) minutes, it would make a total loss of time, on the entire route, of twenty-five (25) hours, or, more than one day. If each one loses ten (10) minutes, it would make a total loss of sixteen and one half (16½) hours, or, the best part of a day.

On the contrary, if each driver gains that amount of time, it leaves a margin of time against accidents and some delays.

All hands will see the great necessity of promptness and dispatch; every minute of time is valuable as the Company are under heavy forfeit if the mail is behind time.

Conductors must note the hour and date of departure from Stations, the causes of delay, if any, and all particulars. They must also report the same fully to their respective Superintendents.

* The Station referred to on Gila River, is 40 miles west of Maricopa Wells.

JOHN BUTTERFIELD.
*Pres't.*

Butterfield's Overland Mail Company's schedules listed the Potts Inn as a home station stop. It is estimated that Butterfield Stages stopped at the Inn over 300 times in the period that the line operated in the state of Arkansas. A mounting rock in the front yard would have served for the ladies to step from the stage. *Author's collection.*

A section of the Old Military Road east of the Hurricane swing station (east of Atkins)  remains unchanged by time.  The view of the road today would probably appear much as it would have looked to the Butterfield driver in the stagecoach era.

If you listen closely, you can almost hear the hooves of the horses and the wheels of the stagecoach as it traveled the road. *Author's collection*

A postal desk sits in the wide hallway through the center of Potts Inn Museum.  As postmaster for Galley Creek, Kirkbride special ordered this postal desk to be placed in his new home. It traveled from New Orleans up the Mississippi River to the Arkansas River then finally to the town of Galla Rock where it was loaded on a wagon and delivered to Potts Inn.  This desk would have been used for mail from the Butterfield's Overland Mail Company's stagecoach from 1858-1861, as well as U. S. Mail after the Butterfield time.  In the storage compartment of this historic desk is a copy of the 1847 Laws and Regulations of the Post Office Department. *Author's collection.*

October 9, 1858

Sir:

"Your dispatch has been received.  I cordially congratulate you upon the results.  It is a glorious triumph for civilization and the Union.  Settlements will soon follow the course of the road, and the East and West will be bound together by a chain of living Americans, which can never be broken."

Telegram from President James Buchanan to John Butterfield

On November 19, 1869, John Butterfield died and is buried in the Forest Hill cemetery in Utica, New York.  Other members of the team that created the stagecoach trail also rest in  upstate New York. This incredible man created a mail delivery system that transformed the nation's mail service and connected the many Americans living in California to their loved ones in the East.  Although the Civil War and the ensuing financial and travel chaos resulted in the closure of the southern route of the stagecoach trail in 1861, Butterfield performed an almost impossible feat and should be regarded as an American hero.  Potts Inn at Pottsville was a part of that extraordinary time. *Courtesy of Gerald Ahnert.*

On October 10, 1958 a one hundred year celebration was held all along the three thousand mile route. A special stamp was issued by the U. S. Postal Service in honor of this day and a plaque was placed on the northeast chimney of the Potts home. *Author's collection.*

Potts' Station on Butterfield Overland Mail Route from Memphis to Fort Smith. The house was built in 1850's by Kirkbride Potts and has been occupied by the family continuously to the present. It is located in Pope County, at Pottsville. Photo made 1956.

In 1958, a sixteen page booklet was published by the Arkansas Butterfield Overland Mail Centennial Committee. The history of the Potts Inn is on page 15 of the booklet. *Courtesy of the 1958 Butterfield Overland Mail Route Centennial Booklet by W.J. Lemke and Ted R Worley.*

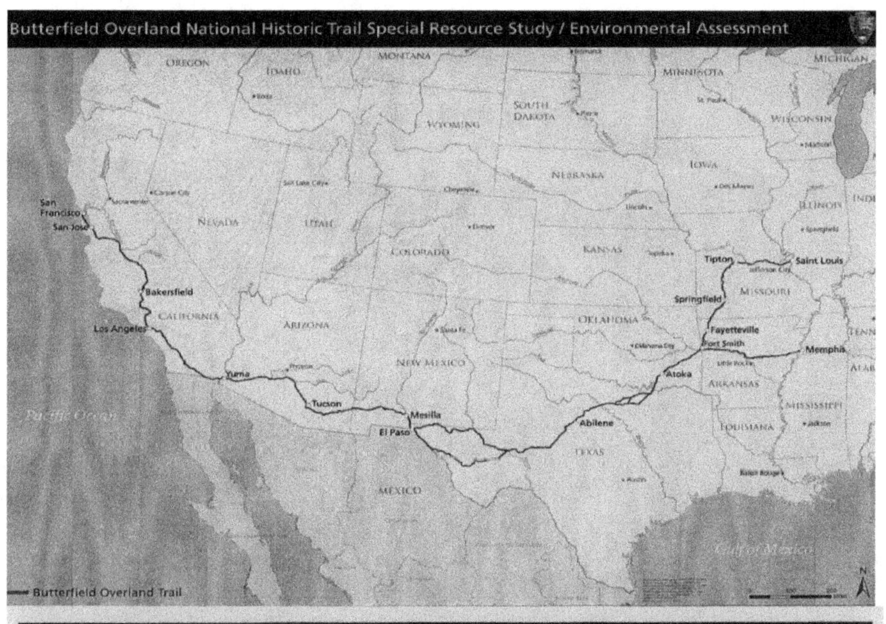


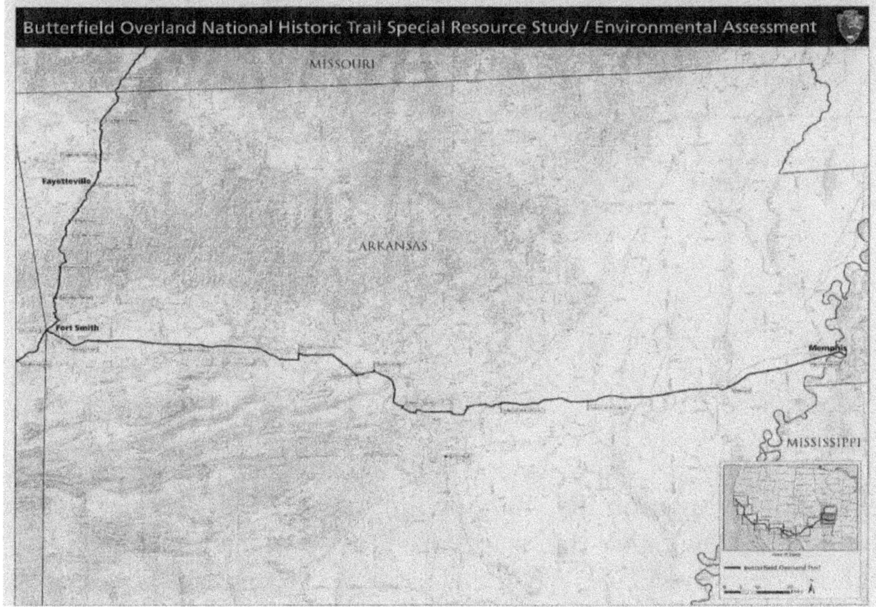


Maps shown include the Arkansas and National sections of the Butterfield Overland Mail trail proposed to be named as a National Historic Trail. *Courtesy of Arkansas Senator John Boozman.*

In 2007 Arkansas Congressman John Boozman introduced legislation for a feasibility study by the National Park Service of Butterfield's Overland Mail stagecoach trail designation as a National Historic Trail. When that study was complete, Senator Boozman introduced SB4404 in the U S Senate on August 3, 2020 to designate this important stagecoach mail route as a National Historic Trail. This sign located at the Pottsville railroad overpass marks this historic trail. *Author's collection.*

In the Fall of 1861 during the hectic early days of the Civil War, a telegraph wire was used to connect Little Rock and Fort Smith. Located in front of the Morton-Thompson home on the old Military Road about a mile west of the Potts Inn, this last remaining support for the telegraph wire was struck by lightning in 2015 and is nearly gone today. The Butterfield stagecoaches would have passed this tree more than 300 times, four times weekly, traveling east and west from 1858-1861. *Author's collection.*

# Early Pottsville Churches

## Methodist

The early Methodist Church, school and cemetery were at Bradley Cove .  The Potts and Logan family were living in the area in 1828, so this would have been the earliest place for church and school. Later the church  moved to Potts Station. In 1873, a two-story white structure named King's Chapel was built  north of the railroad track. The Methodist Episcopal used the downstairs for services while the Pottsville Masons used the upstairs for their meetings.

During the turmoil before the Civil War, in 1844 the Methodist Episcopal Church became divided. This division affected many churches in the nation, and for years, Pottsville had two Methodist Churches. A Pottsville Methodist Church South was established on the northwest corner of current Ash Street and Highway 331.

In 1913 a new Methodist Episcopal Church was built on the east side of River Road south of the railroad tracks.  It burned in 1927. Money was scarce.  Necessity led the minister and members of the congregation to complete the construction.  The church was completed in 1928.

In 1939, after more than ninety years of division, the two Methodist churches joined to become the Pottsville Methodist Episcopal Church.  The 1928 church building was used by the merged congregation.

## Presbyterian

The founders of the Associate Reformed Presbyterian church migrated in the 1850's to Arkansas from western North Carolina, bound tightly together by family ties, their Reformed faith, and a fierce love of freedom and opportunity, they flourished in this pioneer community. They established Pisgah Church, school and cemetery in 1853 and later, the Bethany Church, three miles south of town. No known photos exist of the Pisgah Church, but a drawing represents the old frame church.  A marble memorial marks the site today.  In 1884, services at Pisgah were discontinued, and the congregation constructed a new church at Potts Station.  The new church was completed about 1906 just east of the current parsonage.

After that building burned, a new beautiful brick building was built and consecrated in February 1917.  It and served the congregation until it was also destroyed by fire in 1959. The Pottsville Associate Reformed Church remains located at the corner of today's East Ash and River Road in the building constructed in 1960. The Bethany Church merged with the Pottsville congregation in the 1960s.

## Baptist

The founders of the Baptist Church met on October 13, 1883 and adopted the articles of faith of the church covenant.  In January 1913 a building commission purchased one and three-fourths acres of land for $166 from A. H. Boggess for a building site.  The question of whether the structure would be constructed of brick or wood was raised at a meeting of the commission on March 23, 1913.  A vote of 91-7 favored brick construction.  This beautiful structure on the southwest corner of Ash Street and River Road was completed in about 1913.  It served the Baptist congregation for many years.

No photos are known to exist for the Bradley Cove Church and school which was organized by the early Methodist in the area in the 1830's and 1840's.  It was located west of the Potts and Logan families at the foot of Crow Mountain.  A cemetery and a tiny replica of the Bradley Cove Church serve as reminders of the history there. *Author's collection.*

Kings Chapel, built in 1873, was located on the east side of Ash
Street north of the railroad track. The Methodist Episcopal Church
held services downstairs and the Masonic Lodge held meetings
upstairs. The Methodist built a new building in 1913 south of the
railroad tracks, but the Masons continued to use this building for
many more years. *Courtesy of Ray Tucker.*

A new Methodist Church was built in 1913 across the railroad track and directly south of the King' Chapel building.   Dedication of the new church was held September 28, 1913.   The program of the dedication provides a great deal of information about the congregation members, especially the pioneer women and their contributions to the church and community. *Courtesy of Ray Tucker.*

Workmen at the site of the new 1913 church: J. Newt Cloninger, Frank Garren, J. S. Blake, T. N. Parrish. The building description in the dedication program says "white frame building with a modest bell tower and a tiny vestibule which held a small table with church literature". *Courtesy of Ray Tucker.*

Young people in front of Methodist Church:  Boys:  John Rackley, Thurstin Rankin, Raymond Pryor, Brooks Teeter.  Girls:  Lela Walker, Faye Teeter, Rhea King, Hazel Jones, Thelma Rankin, Pluma Robertson, Ada Robinson, Ruth Adams. *Courtesy of Kenneth Taylor.*

The South Methodist Church was located on the northwest corner of Hwy 331 and Ash Street, directly across the street from the Methodist Episcopal Church. This photo shows children and adults heading for Sunday School classes that were held in the basement of the structure. *Courtesy of Kenneth Taylor.*

Group of men at Methodist Church south, at Pottsville about 1927.

*From the Pope County Arkansas History Book Vol. 2*

Ladies Bible Class of the South Methodist Church Pottsville: Row 1:  Nora Teeter, Norma Shue, Mary E. Eoff, Reba Wheeler, Ora Teeter, Lizzie Teeter, Velma Motley, Ruth Beaty.  Row 2:  3rd person, Mrs. Wes Pryor, Gertie Teeter, Gladys Baker, Ursley Owens, ? Teeter.  Row 3:  2nd person Allie Blake. *Courtesy of Kenneth Taylor.*

Pottsville Children Bible Class was held at the Methodist Church. The teachers were Wanda Taylor and Christina Ferguson. The children were from the area churches and community. *Courtesy of Kenneth Taylor.*

When Presbyterian pioneers came to Pope County in 1851, they soon established a church, school, and cemetery in an area they named Pisgah after the church they had left in the Carolinas. No photograph is known to exist of the Pisgah Church, which was the original site for Associate Reformed worship in the River Valley.

This drawing is the only known rendering of the early church and school building. *Courtesy of Rev. Howard Wheeler, Pottsville Associated Reformed Presbyterian Church.*

Located on the highest point of the Pisgah Cemetery is a marble monument.  It was erected by the Associate Reformed Presbyterian Church and recognizes the perseverance of those first brave men and women who settled here so long ago.  Pisgah  is a large active cemetery on both the north and south side of Pisgah Road about 3 miles west of Pottsville.

When you stand on this spot, there is a clear view of Mt. Nebo, also a biblical name for this beautiful mountain across the Arkansas River.

*Author's collection.*

The coming of the railroad in the 1870's triggered the shift of Pottsville's population and town center closer to the tracks. The frame Associate Reformed Presbyterian Church was built at Potts Station in 1884. The meeting of the General Synod of the Associate Reformed Presbyterian Church convened here in 1888. At that meeting, the Board of Home Missions--now Outreach North America was chartered.

This photograph was taken around 1906 and was the gift of Mrs. J.W. (Ruth) Carson of Gastonia, N.C.. The Presbyterian Manse is seen to the right. *Courtesy of Rev. Howard Wheeler, Pottsville Associated Reformed Presbyterian Church.*

Bethany Presbyterian Church was located about three miles south of Pottsville on River Road.  The church and school was established around the time the first Potts Station Presbyterian Church was built, c. 1884.  When Bethany was built, worship at Pisgah church was discontinued and the congregation divided between Bethany and Pottsville.  This photo shows the Church that was built in 1948. Members moved to the Pottsville Church and services were discontinued at Bethany in the 1960s. *Courtesy of Rev. Howard Wheeler, Pottsville Associated Reformed Presbyterian Church.*

The second Pottsville Associate Reformed Presbyterian Church was built after the original Potts Station church burned. This beautiful brick building with stained glass windows and columns on the front was completed in 1917 and stood on the corner of Ash Street (the Old Military Road) and the River Road. It was consecrated in February 1917 and served the Presbyterian congregation until 1959 when it burned and was replaced by the present structure.

The entire property is adjacent to the historic antebellum Potts Inn. *Courtesy of Rev. Howard Wheeler, Pottsville Associated Reformed Presbyterian Church.*

Founders of the Pottsville Baptist Church organized in 1883 and met at the site of their first church building a mile east of Pottsville.  In 1886 the church became the Potts Station Baptist Church and then, when Pottsville was incorporated in 1897, it became the Pottsville Baptist Church.

When completed In 1913, this beautiful brick building was the largest Baptist Church in Arkansas.  *Courtesy of David Duffield, photo belonged to his Dad, Ronnie Duffield.*

Left side of Pottsville Baptist Congregation.  Probably early 1960's.
*Courtesy of Rev. Jim Huffman, Pottsville Baptist Church.*

Right side of Baptist Congregation.  Probably early 1960's.
*Courtesy of Rev. Jim Huffman, Pottsville Baptist Church.*

Potluck meal enjoyed at the Baptist church. *Courtesy of Rev. Jim Huffman, Pottsville Baptist Church.*

The four Pottsville Churches were all located on the corners of then Hwy 64(Ash Street) and River Road.

Adam Ford was baptized by Pastor R. D. Hester in Galla Creek on land owned by Ford's nephew, Ronnie Duffield. The area was north of Hwy 64, close to present day water reservoir.

For generations, this area was a popular spot for swimming, baptisms, and revivals. A brush arbor provided shade during revivals. *Courtesy of David Duffield.*

May 1962 Carolyn Duffield-Dale Kendrick  wedding party is one of the only known wedding photos in the 1913 church.

The wedding party included  bridesmaids Linda Duffield and Linda Kendrick with maid of honor being Margaret Duffield Taylor. The best man was Johnny Strickland, and the groomsmen were Wayne Jones and Jimmy Sparks.  The flower girl was Glenna Taylor, and Ricky Taylor was the ring bearer.  Young groomsmen were Randy Duffield and Larry Duffield and Pastor Herman Hurd. *Courtesy of David Duffield.*

# Early Pottsville Schools

Early buildings often served both as school and church.  The earliest school was a part of the Methodist Church at Bradley Cove (1840's.)  It was located only around the mountain ridge from the Kirkbride Potts family, the Logans and other early settlers.

No known photos exist from the Old Log Potts Station school, but it was located on the site of the current Pottsville Softball Park.  The road ran on the south side of the park and connected to the road to Pisgah cemetery.

The Pisgah school was located next to the 1852 Associate Reformed Presbyterian Pisgah Church west of Pottsville.  Today a large cemetery continues to serve the community where this building once stood.  A large memorial marker recognizes the early history here.

The Presbyterian congregation also built the Bethany school and church 3 miles south  of Pottsville on River Road in 1877.  As all children walked to school in those times, a school had to be located within walking distance.  The names of Pisgah and Bethany were reminders of the communities left behind in North and South Carolina.

The second Potts Station School was built in 1894 about 150 feet northwest of the present day Pottsville Baptist Church on Highway 331.

In 1913 a new large two story brick High School was completed between the first two Pottsville schools on the main road south to the Arkansas River.  This building served the high school students for many years.

Excess buildings from Camp Robinson at the end of World War II provided buildings for Home Economics, Agriculture and cafeteria for the school district.

The stone gym was built in the late 1930's by the WPA.  It took a couple of years to build and was a huge improvement for the school and the students that used it.

No known photos exist from the early school of Bradley Cove or the original Potts Station School. This 1900 photo shows the school that was located just past the current Baptist Church on Ash Street. It appears that there was a well with a covered roof in the front of the school with clapboard siding.

It was common in those days to use a local photo for postcards. The above image is of a postcard sent from Pottsville to Russellville. The postcard was sent from Alice Boggan Dickey to her sister-in-law, Lillie Carpenter Boggan with the following words on the back: "Hello Lillie, How are you getting along these windy days. I heard that the children had been sick hope they are better by this time we are all well. I want to come up there but they use the horses all the time so I don't get to come. I think you ought to come here?" The postage on the card was 1 cent. *Courtesy of Debbie Byrd.*

1910 Pottsville school group (above) and 1912 Pottsville school group (below) pictured in front the school when it was located past the Baptist Church on Ash Street. *Courtesy of the Pottsville School District.*

Built in 1913, this large two-story high school was a wonderful building for its time.  A wide set of stairs located on the front side of the building was used as an :up" staircase.  A second set of stairs at the rear of the building served as a "down" staircase.

Many stories are told of Halloween pranks in Pottsville. Mischievous students would take apart a farm wagon and carry the pieces to the second floor and then put it back together on the roof for it to be discovered the next day. *Courtesy of the Pottsville School District.*

Photograph was taken on April 26, 1917 of the Pottsville Girls' Basketball Team.  From left to right:  Nola King, Thelma Hamilton, Mary Dickey, Prof. Reece A. Caudle, Salemma Blake, Lora King, Carrie Williams.

The girls' basketball team of Pottsville High School was the pride of the student body.  They engaged in five games during the term, meeting defeat but once.  They defeated Russellville, Dardanelle and Atkins twice. *Courtesy of Kenneth Taylor, son of Thelma Hamilton.*

This photo is Ishmuel Jones Pottsville football player in 1921. *Courtesy of the Pottsville School District.*

The 1921 Pottsville boys football team. Members of the 1921 team were from left: first row-- L.D. Manning, Otto Walker, Roe Yow, Ottis McNutt and Sid Adams. Second row--Harold Jones, James May, Ralph Robertson and Burl Pryor. Third row--Mignon Martin, Scott Ewing, Ishmael Jones, Coach Roland Pryor, Oda McNutt and Harold Boggess. *Courtesy of the Pottsville School District.*

Pottsville student body in front of the Pottsville High School in 1921. *Courtesy of the Pottsville School District.*

Pottsville Girls basketball team in 1921.  Estelle Martin, Faye Rockley Onsbey, Ellie Brashears, Lucille Robertson, Bernice Oates, Lady Evelyn Martin. *Courtesy of the Pottsville School District.*

1922 Pottsville Boys Basketball team.  Members unidentified.
*Courtesy of the Pottsville School District.*

1926 Pottsville Football Team (above).  *Courtesy of the Pottsville School District.*
1926 Class of Pottsville High School (below).  *Courtesy of Tom Teeter.*

Pottsville School students in 1929  First row:  Marie Rogers, Mildred Bradford, Dana Kinslow, Eunice Kendrick, Ruby Staggs, Mary Jane Daniels, Mary Ruth Cloniger , Ila Ferguson, Ines, Shues, Ruby Jane Steward, Lois Staggs, Helen McClain, Inez Peruin, Reva Keene.  Second row:  Wheeler Robertson, Norman Bradford, Milton Rockley, Swain Thompson, Raymond Kendrick, Robert Teeter, Brooks Morphis, Robert Motley, ? Curtis, Forrest Henry Jr., Miss Cole, Otto McGuire, Mackie Taylor.  Third row:  Ada Ruth Robertson, G B. Robertson, Morton Rankin, Rayburn Kendrick, Velma Owens, Brown Pervine, Laurell Morphis, Charles Loveless, Silas Teeter, Robert Daniels, Robert McGuire and Joe A. Jones
*Courtesy of Pottsville School District*

Clifford and Clyde Hamaker pose in front of Pottsville's first school bus purchased in 1930.  Clifford attended the Bethany School which offered education through the 8th grade.  Once done, he stayed and retook classes for two more years.  At the age of sixteen, he was offered a job driving the new bus and he accepted.  He probably did not have his license at that time, but he drove safely and no harm came of it.  *Courtesy of Linda Hamaker Reasoner.*

Pottsville Seniors in 1931.  Class members from left:  Ada Reed, Lorene Smith, Faye Bowden, Ruth Teeter, Lillian Prior, Helen Adams, Vestal McNutt, Ruth Taylor and Mary Ellen Teeter.  Back row, Raymond Boggess, Edward Baker, Jim Chronister, Porter and Ivan Pullen. *Courtesy of the Pottsville School District.*

1933 Pottsville High School Junior Class. *Courtesy of the Pottsville School District.*

1934 Pottsville High School Class. *Courtesy of the Pottsville School District.*

1940 Pottsville High School Senior Class. Row one: Martha Lon Ferguson, Marjorie Teeter, Arletta Teeter, Eula Rackley, Ida Lee Robertson, Verdelle Bowden, Virginia Sue Radman, Ruth Ellen Falls. Row two: George Jones, Helen Robinson, Sybil Roberts, Anna Lee Dunn, Virginia Ruth Teeter, Ava Hilda Choate, Bernice Owens, Estelle Staggs, Ina Dell. Row three: J A Motley, Lloyd Morton, Robert Jones, Robert Peters, Franklin Oates, Clarence Rackley, Paul Robertson, J W Sanders, Billy Taylor, S C Tucker. *Courtesy of the Pottsville School District.*

1944 Pottsville Schools Seventh Grade Class and , below early elementary building. *Courtesy of the Pottsville School District.*

The high school stone gymnasium was built in the late 1930's as a Pottsville project of the Works Progress Association (WPA).  WPA was often referred to jokingly as "We piddle around."  Kenneth Taylor remembers his father, Weaver was the foreman of the gymnasium project.  He said the rocks used came from Galla Creek, starting at the foot of Crow Mountain.  Probably a five mile stretch of Galla Creek was needed to provide the amount of stone required to build such a large building.

The new gym must have been a welcome addition for basketball players.  Previous to the new gym's construction, students had played outside on a flat piece of ground adjacent to the site of the new gym.  The new building had wide comfortable bleachers for basketball spectators, restrooms and dress-out rooms for boys and girls.  An exciting game played in this gym in 1968 gave the Senior boys basketball team a berth in the State tournament.

A concession stand, shining court floor and a trophy display case were also a part of this wonderful building.  Beautiful stage curtains, with a large "P" on them, were closed during games but opened to display dramatic backgrounds for school plays and graduations.  It served as the center of school activity during its lifetime.  *Author's collection.*

In the 1940's after World War II had ended, the military had many buildings for which it had no need.  This structure was used on the Pottsville High School campus as the agricultural building after being moved from Camp Robinson in North Little Rock.  *Courtesy of Pottsville School District.*

The Home Economics Building was also moved from Camp Robinson after the end of World War ll.  It served for many years as the Home Economics building for girls.  *Courtesy of the Pottsville School District.*

The top image on this page feature the school cafeteria, which was located between the elementary and the new High School building. (A portion of the elementary can be seen on the right.) The bottom photograph shows the High School building in 1950 when it had been in use for more than thirty years. It was replaced in the 1960's with a more modern building. Notice the large cedar trees in front. *Courtesy of the Pottsville School District.*

Pottsville Elementary School around 1950. *Courtesy of the Pottsville School District.*

This photo was taken when several of the first buildings of the school campus were still in place: the agriculture and home economics buildings and the stone gym were all still standing. Shown in the background is the new high school. *Author's collection.*

Arch built by the Class of 1932.  Boys included:  Kermit Tucker, Clifford Hamaker, Raymond King, Jones Kinslow, and Robert Brown. Girls included:  Nell Teeter, Edna Robertson, Martha Teeter, Erma Wiliker, Hazel Falls.  *Author's collection.*

Image of Rocky Point School with Bud and Jane Peters standing in the school doorway and Burgess Jones driving the mules. This photograph was taken just before the teardown began in 1950. *Courtesy of Kenneth Taylor.*

The Pleasant Grove School pictured on September 20, 1894. It was located about 5 miles south of Pottsville. *Courtesy of the Pope County Historical Foundation.*

In 1877, the Associate Reformed Presbyterian Church recognized that the area south of Pottsville on River Road needed a school and church located there.  The Bethany Church served the area until the last services were held in 1960.

The two photos from 1907 and 1912 would have been from the Bethany School about 3 miles from Potts Station.  *Courtesy of the Pottsville School District.*

Class of Bethany School 1919-1920:  All students are not identified. Seated:  Louia Tucker Ferguson, Terral Kessler, Row 2:  Erma Kessler, Grover Harris, Verna Stewart, Ruth Workman, Floy Jones, Lola Tucker, Lettie Tucker, Row 3:  #2 John Stewart, May Workman (girl with hat) #10 H.O. Walker, Justin in front of John, Teacher in back far left, Ethel Rackley, girls with identical checked dresses, Flora and Laura Parker, girl next to them in checked dress, Mamie Kendrick, girl on next row back in checked dress, Ruth Oates, girl next to her in dark dress with white collar, Lois Stewart Robertson, girl next to her far right, Mary Workman Kessler, behind them the tall boy is Clarence Cline, next tallest boy is Claude Workman and boy standing with hands on window sill is Dow Morton. *Courtesy of the Pottsville School District.*

Still standing today is the South New Hope School built by the WPA that consolidated with Pottsville in 1949.  Below is the Mt. Zion School and along with Old Cove, Norris Chapel, Pleasant Grove, Bethany, Rocky Point, Double Springs, Mars Hill and Maple Springs all became a part of Pottsville School District.

Mt. Zion School — South of Pottsville, 1932.

*From the Pope County Arkansas History Book Vol 1.*

# Early Pottsville Businesses

The Falls-Sinclair General Mercantile offered hats, shoes, yard goods, thread, groceries, farm implements and seed, school textbooks, paper and pencils. A 1936 advertisement describes Falls & Sinclair as "Pottsville's largest and best store--offering almost anything you need." Owners over the years have included the names of Baker, Keener, Chansley, DuVall and Morton.

When the Citizens Bank opened in 1913 the bank had assets of $15,000. A newspaper article from the time describes the bank as follows: "It is a modern new brick building especially designed for the banking business. The walls of the fire-proof vault are 24 inches thick with airspace and on the inside of this vault is an Ely-Morris manganese screw-door safe, which has withstood the test of some of the most notorious burglars in the world. In this connection, the management of the bank extends a cordial invitation to patrons of the bank and their friends to make this a depository of their deeds, collaterals, jewelry and other valuables without charge. Members of the first board of directors included: E.R. Jones, C.R. Teeter, Roy Falls, J.H. Oates, N. E. Owens, A.H. Boggess, and J. B. Sinclair. All of these gentlemen are substantial citizens and business men and are well known for their high sense of good citizenship and reliability in financial affairs."

Among these exceptional men, was Dr. Charles Richard Teeter, the son of James and Ellen Teeter. He married Cora Ann Whitesides in 1908. Charles was a farmer and schoolteacher before entering the University of Louisville medical school in 1904 and as was common at the time, beginning his 36 year medical practice in Pottsville and Russellville. He graduated from the University of Arkansas medical school in 1907 and completed additional study at Tulane University in New Orleans.

He recalled the most trying time was during the flu epidemic of 1918 when hundreds of people lay at the point of death. He once made continuous rounds for three days and nights without a moment's rest. Weather at that time was the worst possible--cold, snow and drizzling rain. To make his house calls Dr. Teeter rode a horse or drove a buggy over roads which became bogs during winter. Later he purchased a Ford automobile for the trips.

Scene with snow is from the 1940's looking east in the Pottsville downtown area. Shown are the Falls-Sinclair general mercantile store and drug store on the right, Citizens Bank and other stores on the left, and the train depot in the distance. Corner of Dr. Teeter's office is on far left of photo.

Snow fall is somewhat unusual in central Arkansas, so always a opportunity for photographs. *Courtesy of Sue Roberts.*

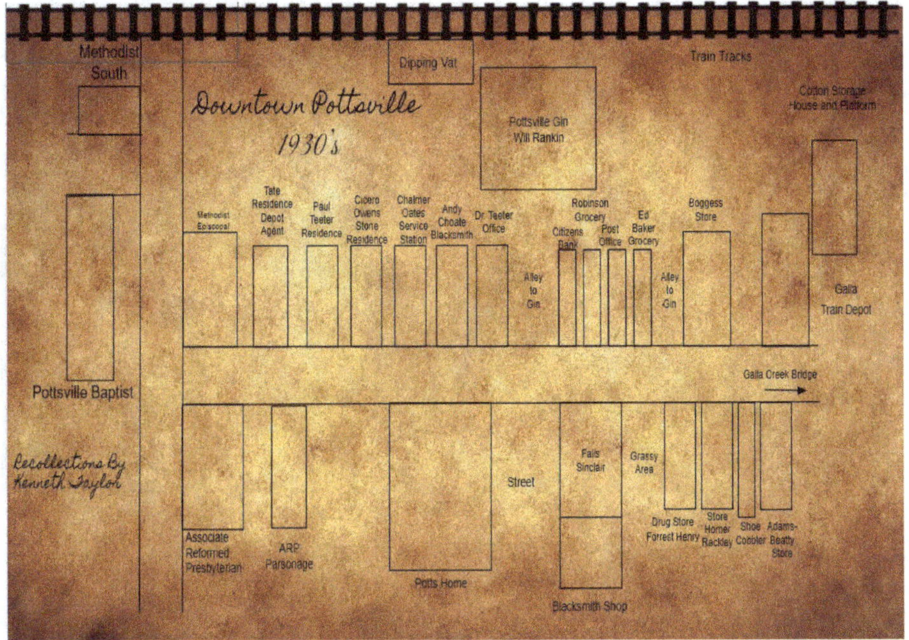


Map of the Pottsville downtown area during the Depression era as remembered by Kenneth Taylor. *Courtesy of Peyton Shewmake, Pottsville High School, EAST.*

Between the Falls-Sinclair and Forrest Henry Drug Store was a grassy area that was used for social events. Charles Oates recalls that he won a Blue Ribbon for his pet rooster at the Pottsville Fair there. Kenneth Taylor tells the story of a Husband Hollering contest. His father Weaver was working down by Galla Creek and his mother Thelma, called out loudly, WEEAAVER!!!! and he came running and she won the contest.

There were ice cream socials held on the grassy area up until the 1960's.

Customer Morphis with Harvey and William Leslie Oates.  The Oates Brothers Store was located just east of Falls-Sinclair store *Courtesy of Melanie Wheeler.*

The Falls-Sinclair store was the first brick building in Pottsville in 1887.  A large structure,  40 x 80 feet, the walls are 3 bricks deep with a beautiful tin ceiling.  Signs still visible show the store as E. B. Falls & Son on the front exterior wall and Falls & Sinclair General Mercantile on the west side.   In 2021, the building is no longer a business, but there are plans to renovate for a community center. *Courtesy of the Charles Oates collection.*

Interior of the Falls-Sinclair store in the 1940's shows the large variety of items for sale.  Shown are Ilah Ferguson, employee John McNutt and co-owner Boyce Sinclair.

It was the place to go for school textbooks, paper and pencils. Everything from clothing, hats, shoes, food items, nails and animal feed was available for sale.  The pot-bellied store in the center of the building was the gathering place for men to visit in the winter.  In the summer they would occupy the "spit and whittle" bench on the front of the store. *Courtesy of the Charles Oates collection.*

Beaty-Adams store was an early Pottsville business. L. Adams stands in the doorway of the store. As a Justice of the Peace, he held traffic court inside also. His business partner, James A Beaty served as Pottsville's first mayor. Mayor Beaty died in 1907. *Courtesy of the city of Pottsville.*

Located in the area between the Citizens Bank and the dipping vat was the large Pottsville Cotton Gin, Will Rankin owner. The gin was powered by a large diesel engine that had to be started by a smaller gasoline engine. East of the depot, a rail spur allowed the large bales of ginned cotton to be loaded directly onto railcars for shipping. Now the area is the home of Rankin Park. *Courtesy of Kenneth Taylor.*

Unidentified man weighing a cotton bale *Courtesy of Pope County Historical Foundation.*

Will and Lillie Rankin family were very active Pottsville citizens and well respected by everyone.  They lived just past the Potts Inn, close to the gin. Stories are told of Mrs. Rankin hosting the local children for refreshments and teaching piano lessons. *Courtesy of the Pope County Historical Foundation*

The Pottsville cattle dipping vat is a concrete structure with an associated dripping platform located at the northwest comer of Rankin Park on East Ash Street.   The vat is about two feet wide and approximately seven feet deep. The Pottsville community was a part of the government effort to eradicate Texas Tick Fever in Arkansas, 1907-1943. All cattle were required to be moved through the solution in the dipping vat to kill the ticks.  The cattle dipping vat is listed on the Historical Register. *Courtesy of Ralph Wilcox, Arkansas Historical Preservation.*

# Citizens Bank

Capital Stock, $15,000.00

Pottsville, Ark.

R. O. MORTON, Pres.          J. B. SINCLAIR, Vice-Pres.
          N. H. BELL, Cashier.

---

# Oates & Pryor,

### First-Class Smith and Repair Shop

Horse-Shoeing a Specialty  :  All kinds of Woodwork

Pottsville, Ark.

---

W. L. Oates.          T. M. Oates.          J. H. Oates.

# Oates Bros.

## General Merchandise

Pottsville, Ark.

---

## E. B. Falls & Son

Dry Goods, Clothing, Boots, Shoes and
General Merchandise

Galla, R. R. Station.          Pottsville, Ark.

---

## Pope County Nursery

### Nursery Stock of All Kinds.

Nursery inspected regularly by State Inspector of Arkansas.   All stock guaranteed true to variety.

Pottsville, Ark.

---

## J. E. Allmon

### Ginner, Miller and Cotton Seed Buyer.

Always pay highest price for White Corn and Cotton Seed.  Your patronage solicited.

Pottsville, Ark.

From the Methodist Episcopal Church dedication program of the new church held on September 28, 1913. The booklet covers the history of the Pottsville Methodist Circuit, the Pastors who had served the church and some of the individual church members. Several pages were dedicated to sponsoring businesses, including Atkins, Russellville and Pottsville merchants. *Courtesy of Ray Tucker and the September 28, 1913 Methodist Episcopal Church Dedication Services Souvenir Program.*

Cashier Neil Bell stands in front of Citizens Bank in 1913. A newspaper article describes the bank: "It is a modern new brick building especially designed for the banking business. The management of the bank extends a cordial invitation to patrons of the bank and their friends to make this a depository of their deeds, collaterals, jewelry, and other valuables without charge." Unlike many other banks, it was able to remain open during the Depression. *Courtesy of the Charles Oates collection.*

This Ely-Norris manganese screw-door safe sits inside the 24 inch fire-proof bank vault. With extra-thick walls, rounded corners, and a time lock system, the cannonball safe was considered "robber proof". In 1922, aspiring bank robbers were able to cut a 24 inch hole in the bank's fire-proof vault, but quickly gave up after encountering the heavy duty safe. *Courtesy of the Charles Oates collection.*

On the day  Citizens Bank opened in 1913, eleven year old Wade Oates was sitting on the steps of Falls-Sinclair store waiting for the new bank to open.  He walked across the street and was the first customer in the door.  He made a deposit of 25 cents.  When the bank closed in 1992, Wade was the last customer to make a withdrawal.  Also pictured is bank teller Cornelia Virden.  This story was written by Charles Oates, son of Wade Oates. *Courtesy of the Charles Oates collection.*

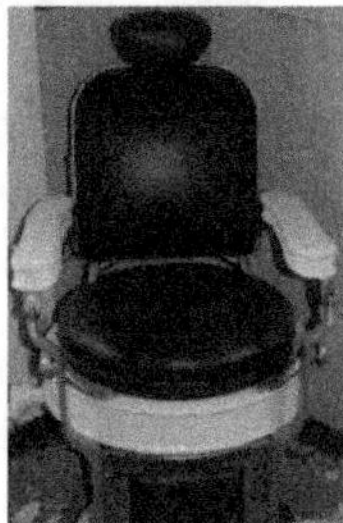

In the early days of Citizens Bank a barber chair sat in the northeast corner of the lobby.  A customer could get a haircut and conduct banking business at the same place.

In 1869, Kirkbride and Pamelia Potts granted the Little Rock and Fort Smith the right-of-way through their property for the sum of $1.00. The train depot was located at the east end of town only a short distance from Potts Inn. This scene was captured sometime in the early 1900s. According to Pottsville citizen Kenneth Taylor, the train came through Pottsville at 5 pm every day. *Courtesy of the City of Pottsville.*

Marvin Cockrum, David B. Oates, Mack Sinclair, and Melvin Cockrum stand in front of the Pottsville Train Depot. *Courtesy of David B. Oates.*

Pottsville Postal Service members. Postmaster H. Guy Oates (in shirtsleeves) stands in the doorway of this early post office as carriers, from left: John Pryor, Charlie Thompson and Charles Blake prepare to deliver the main. Mr. Oates was postmaster from 1913 to 1922. *Courtesy of the City of Pottsville.*

Pottsville blacksmith shop located behind a warehouse at the rear of the Falls Sinclair store.. From left: Joe Pryor, J.Q. Owens and Walter Lollis.
*Courtesy of the City of Pottsville.*

Dr. Teeter's office about 1960 vacant for many years . *Courtesy of Author's collection*

Dr. C. R. Teeter, affectionately known as "Old Doc Charlie" was a practicing physician in Pottsville and the surrounding area for more than three decades.  He drove more than half a million miles and made more than 76,000 house calls. His office was located just west of the present day Rankin City Park. *Courtesy of the Pope County Historical Foundation.*

A traveling photographer took this picture of S.M. Shue's downtown Pottsville Grocery Store and Cafe in 1933. Pictured front row from left: Milton Tucker, Macie Wylie, and S. M. Shue. Back row: Mail Carrier John Pryor, with his mail sack, two unidentified men, James Oates, Hayden Smith, Ivan Pullen, Tom King, Gip Thompson, and two other unidentified men. *Courtesy of Kenneth Taylor.*

The Iron bridge across Galla Creek was completed in 1920, replacing a smaller, but similar bridge located near the railroad. It was removed and replaced by a modern culvert type bridge that would accommodate school buses when the high school relocated to Pine Ridge Road. *Courtesy of David Duffield.*

This service station was located directly across from the Potts home on the north side of Ash Street.  It was built in the early 1920s and was originally a Crown service station operated by Chalmers Oates and G.C. Owens.  Shown in this photo is Chalmer Oates, about 1925. *Courtesy of the Charles Oates collection.*

Shown in this photograph is Haney DuVall at his service station on Hwy 64.  The service station and tourist court were located at the southeast corner of Dr. J. N. Thompson's place on the old Military Road on the road leading to swimming hole. *Courtesy of the Charles Oates collection.*

In about 1950 Dr. J. N. Thompson, wife June and two sons lived in the historic Morton home place located on the Old Military Road. Always interested in poultry, a family photo album contains  a picture of him at age three with a crippled rooster, his pet.  At the age of ten, Thompson's 4-H project involved poultry..
He worked on the college poultry farm and after graduation continued to be interested in poultry.  He conducted poultry research in the early 1940s at a Texas Agriculture Station.  In 1953 he developed a strain of broad breasted white turkey which received national recognition.
Dr. Thompson's hatchery which still stands today. It was an early piece of the total poultry processing industry that integrated hatcheries, feed mills and processing plants.
Dr. Thompson, a Pottsville resident is  to be recognized as an early pioneer in a new industry.  The River Valley, Arkansas, and indeed the nation and the world have been a recipient of his efforts.
*Author's collection.*

Luke Duffield and family hauling shale from Bernice Anthracite Mine #4  near Russellville around 1952.  Tiny, Ronnie Duffield, Carolyn Duffield, Luke Duffield, Linda Duffield and Billy Duffield.

If you look closely you can see Billy's wife, Ernestine Duffield looking out the passenger's side window. *Courtesy of David Duffield*

The oldest business in Pottsville was Potts Inn.  Completed in 1858, the same year as the running of the Butterfield's Overland Mail Company's stagecoach first run, it continued for many years providing lodging and food for travelers.

Even today, as a museum it operates as a business in downtown Pottsville, still continuing to welcome visitors and share its history. *Courtesy of the Pope County Historical Foundation.*

# Community

Traditionally, a community referred to a group of people who lived in the same geographically area.  However, experience tells us that community is more than sharing the same place.  Communities share a common purpose, background, or interest that creates a sense of cohesion and belonging.

In the early days, the River Valley was sparsely populated.  Location played a large role in the establishment of communities.  Life on the frontier could be merciless.  Neighbors depended on one another especially in rural areas.  Being a part of a community could be the difference between life and death.   Survival and protection were a common purpose that united many early settlers.

Just as sharing burdens makes them lighter, sharing joys makes them all the more sweet, and the people of Pottsville shared many joys.  Gatherings were special.  Many of the big celebrations and events were reported and recorded in newspapers.  Holidays were special for everyone and celebrated together publicly as well as in the home.

Smaller gatherings are remembered fondly as well.  Saturday evening would be spent with neighbors playing music and singing.  Churches held "socials" where ice cream or ice cold watermelon would be served.  High school seniors knew at least one family in the area would throw a graduation party for all to enjoy.

Through it all, it was the people and the families who settled in Pottsville that really created the community here.  The Potts family may have been one of the first to settle in the area, but many successful hardworking families quickly set down roots that have lasted for generations.

# Circus To Perform at Potts Inn October 20, 1858

Lions and tigers and bears, oh my!  Leopards, Monkeys, Birds, Clowns, Acrobats, Jesters, Jokers, Men of strength and agility. Performing Horses, Miss Albertine, the Young, Fascinating and Beautiful Equestrienne, Bands, Dancers and Little Harry the Infant Tumbler.  Admission 50 cents, children and servants 25 cents at the Potts.  This would have been one month after the first Butterfield stagecoach run.. *Courtesy of Bob Crossman*

# Soiree Of The Season
## Nov. 2, 1882 Newspaper Clipping

Unquestionably the most charming social event of the season was the soiree at the Potts' mansion, Galla Creek Station, on last Tuesday evening, the affair assuming the phase of an impromptu reception in honor of the newly wedded couple, **Mr. Jeff Davis** and bride, nee Ina McKenzie of Russellville.

First of all, the evening was scarcely short of what we might imagine an evening in Fairy-land to be—bright with the silvery moonbeams from full-faced Luna, smiling from her orb on high; balmy with the rich and mellow autumnal air; fresh and bracing in the purity of an atmosphere clear, and soft, and bright; and lastly musical and resonant with the ringing laughter of many merry couples as they gleefully chatted and laughed and sang on their way over the six-mile drive from town to Galla creek.

The road was just in its best plight and as the gay party sped lightly over the smooth prairie, even the hills and mountains which gird the prairie round about, like margin closing in some placid lake, seemed to clap their hands and nod their heads in salutation to the merry cavalcade as they dashed along.

The Potts' mansion has long been known far and wide as the home hospitality and good cheer; and as the merry-makers drew near, the brightly illuminated halls and parlors threw out a light from many a door and window, inviting on, with outstretched arms, the evening's guests.

Once within the spacious parlor jest and repartee and gayety and laughter ruled the hour.  Surely the most gallant beaux and charming belles in the land were there, and without the slightest thing to mar the mirthful measure of time's flight all went a merry as a marriage bell until ten o'clock, when with a kind of fairy enchantment-like change the music and card tables gave way for stand of rarest cakes and lemonades, and the estimable hostess invited all to a repast as rare and elegant as the occasion itself.

'Twas 12 o'clock, or near, when the merry throng began to take their leave.  To the attentive hostess of the evening, Mrs. R.B. Potts, assisted by Mrs. Jamison and Mrs. Davis, the guests, each and all, fell under a debt of gratitude for the splendid time they had enjoyed.


*Soiree of the season, November 2, 1882.  Reception at the Potts Inn in honor of the marriage of Jeff Davis and Ina McKenzie of Russellville.  Jeff Davis would later become Governor of Arkansas. Courtesy of Pope County Historical Foundation*

This unidentified group at Bradley Cove appear to be having a great time.  Bradley Cove was one of the earliest areas settled with a church, school and cemetery.

The Potts family would have lived just around the mountain ridge from there and the Galla Creek swimming hole was popular for generations as a fun place to gather. *Courtesy of Kenneth Taylor.*

Mr. Jason Steggall was a early member and deacon of the Pottsville Methodist Church.  It was said that he fought for both the North and the South during the Civil War.  His grave stone at Pisgah is marked for the Confederate Sons of America.  *Courtesy of Kenneth Taylor.*

Elbert Sleeker and five of his children: Back, L. to R.: Ephrain, John, Homer. Front: Mary Ann, Elbert and Emily.

Elbert Sleeker (son of George and Edey Sleeker) and family.
*Courtesy of Debbie Byrd.*

George and Edey Sleeker settled on land east of Pottsville on the Military Road March 12, 1840. When the Sinclair family arrived in 1855, after more than a decade with no neighbors, they gave the Sinclair family 40 acres where they built their two-story house. Later, the Sinclairs paid back the 40 acres.

Helen Sleeker, daughter of John Sleeker.
*Courtesy of Debbie Byrd.*

Founded in 1890, the Woodmen of the World is a not-for-profit fraternal benefit society that at one time offered grave monuments to families of deceased members.

This large gathering for William Oates (1868-1908) was held in his honor.  His stone is located on the south side of the north section between the two drives at Pisgah cemetery.  *Courtesy of Debbie Byrd.*

This Woodsman of the World sword is on display in the Gentlemen's Parlor at the Potts Inn.  Unknown donor of this item. *Courtesy of Pope County Historical Foundation*

Sarah E. Oates with her decorative fan.  There were many Teeter and Oates family members in the early Pottsville community. *Courtesy of the Pope County Historical Foundation.*

Sarah E. Oates (Mrs. T. M.) with her daughters in Bernice and Marie about 1911. *Courtesy of Charles Oates collection.*

1st Lt. Franklin Bonner Oates served in World War I. *Courtesy of David Bonner Oates.*

*Courtesy of Kenneth Taylor.*

Weaver Taylor and Doyle Baker enjoying a ride in their buggy about 1918. *Courtesy of Kenneth Taylor, son.*

Will Kessler stands in front of his barn with his daughter Erma's prize cow in 1918.  The Kessler's home was three miles south of Pottsville on River Road.  It was later the Frank Wheeler place and the house still stands today. *Courtesy of Kenneth Taylor.*

Clarence and Lois Allmon seated in front of their home.
*Courtesy of the Charles Oates collection.*

Wave Teeter with Franklin Oates. *Courtesy of the Pope County Historical Foundation.*

Clarence and Louise Martin and three children. *Courtesy of the Pope County Historical Foundation.*

Clarence and Louise Martin with three children. *Courtesy of the Pope County Historical*

John and Ava Morton with their mother. *Courtesy of the Pope County Historical Foundation.*

The Oates Family. Row 1: Charles, Lillian, Franklin. Row 2. Marie, Bernice, Sarah E. Row 3. Nina, Eunice. Row 4. Wade, Knop. *Courtesy of the Charles Oates collection.*

James Blake and son Harold  on Ash Street. the main street in
Pottsville leading downtown.  The image was taken on the north
side of Ash Street looking west.  The Presbyterian manse and the
beautiful Presbyterian Church, which was built in 1917 is in the
background.  Notice the electrical poles that look like they were
made from tree trunks.  *Courtesy of Charles Oates collection.*

Cotton wagon was driven by Monroe Davis. The boys in the wagon
are David B. Oates and Mack Sinclair. *Courtesy of David B. Oates*

William Oates and others with their fox dogs are preparing for a fox hunt. *Courtesy of David B. Oates*

Charles Ross Barefield 3rd from left, Robert P Barefield Sr. 4th from Left, Dan Barefield at end on right, Ernest Keener, Jim Whitesides, and a member of the Carpenter family are also pictured. *Courtesy of Debbie Byrd.*

Doctor Charles Richard Teeter and wife Cora
*Drawings courtesy of Tom Teeter*

The Teeter family had settled in Pottsville area during the mid 1840s,. James and Ellen married in 1870 and had 11 children, 9 living to adulthood. At one point, they had more than 35 grandchildren growing up together in the Pottsville area. James was described in his obituary as a "prominent and industrious farmer, an honest and upright citizen."James and Ellen were buried at Pisgah cemetery along with many of their descendants.

Allie Blake with children Salemma, Fred, Charles, Nina and Floyd.
*Courtesy of Charles Oates collection*

G.W. Robertson and wife Sallie Smith Robertson

Lived in the pre-Civil War home built by Captain Silas Parker
*From the Pope County Arkansas History Book vol.1.*

Oates family.  L to R: Girl in front, Ruby, girl in back, Elsie, Father William Leslie, boy in front, Franklin Bonner, Mother Harriet Madrid Reed and Violet Grace Oates.  Their youngest son, Chalmers is not pictured. *Courtesy of David B. Oates*

Young Ladies posing in front of the E.B. Falls & Son General
Mercantile.  On the Left is Forrest O'Daniel Oates, wife of F.B.
Oates  as she visits with friends in downtown Pottsville. *Courtesy of
David B. Oates*

Emma Lollis and Veloa Owens.
House located on north side of
railroad tracks      *Courtesy of
Charles Oates collection*

James Silas Blake and Charles Blake, Jr. *Courtesy of Kenneth Taylor*

## Newspaper article from November 4, 1915

Miss Mary Potts entertained the young people of Pottsville and surrounding country with a Halloween Party Monday night.  There were 87 present.  At 7 o'clock the crowd started from C.S. Carter's on a hobo trip.  At Mr. Carter's each one was presented with a sack of popcorn and from there they went to  J.A. Rackley's where they received a sandwich in a sack.  From there they went to the Rev. C.H. Sherman's where they were run off with a shot gun, then to C.C. Baker's where each one was given an apple in a sack; from there to J.W. McNutt's where each was given something in a sack.  Then all returned to Mrs. A. J. Potts' garret, where the hostess had scattered hay all over the floor and had cornstalks and pea lay along the walls.  There the crowd enjoyed their hobo lunch after which games were played until 10:30 when the crowd returned to their homes.

*Courtesy of Pope County Historical Foundation.*

**Mary Bradford Potts**
**"Aunt Mamie"**

Ava Morton Harris with her new $300 car. *Courtesy of Kenneth Taylor*

May Day dancers on the front lawn of the Potts Inn. Notice the Falls-Sinclair store in background which still stands. *Courtesy of Charles Oates collection.*

Hugh Hall and Floyd Blake. *Courtesy of Kenneth Taylor.*

Tom Falls planting potatoes. *Courtesy of Charles Oates collection*

The Galla Creek bridge was a popular place for gathering.  The bridge drew couples, friends, and anyone looking for a nice spot to visit, swim, or fish. This unidentified  group of young ladies is posing in front of their 1924 Chevrolet. *Courtesy of the   Charles Oates collection.*

Easter egg hunt at Potts Inn.  *Courtesy of the Charles Oates collection*

The Duffield Family photograph including Luke, Mary, Ronnie, and Carolyn. *Courtesy of David Duffield.*

Walter and Luke Duffield. *Courtesy of David Duffield.*

Girls playing.  *Courtesy of Kenneth Taylor*

Girls downtown.  *Courtesy of Kenneth Taylor.*

Harold Blake with dog. *Courtesy of Charles Oates collection*

Brothers Kenneth and Raymond Taylor
*Courtesy of Kenneth Taylor*

Left to Right: Lois Teeter Martin, Sarah E. Teeter Oates, John Teeter, and "Molly" Teeter Talley. *Courtesy of the Pope County Historical Foundation.*

Mr. Wade Oates standing in front of his home.

In the background, his parent's home is visible.
*Courtesy of the Pope County Historical Foundation.*

Pottsville Boy Scout Troup #64--Members W. D. Teeter, Wade A. Oates, B. B. Bevens, Paul W. Teeter and Scoutmaster C.H. Harvison and Assistant Scoutmaster George Jones 1943. *Courtesy of Charles Oates collection*

Irene and Claude Robinson married on September 20, 1941. *Courtesy of Charles Oates collection.*

Major Curtice H Rankin killed in action in France in 1944  The son of W.H. and Lillie Morton Rankin, he was a descendent of two pioneer families.  *From the Pope County History Book Vol. 2.*

Charles Oates (Dec. 21, 1925-Mar 2, 2015) standing between his great, grandparents Thomas and Melissa Oates  grave markers at Pisgah cemetery.  He told the story of them during the Civil War which follows:

*Author's collection.*

From the book, <u>They Sought a Land--A Settlement in the Arkansas River Valley 1840-1870</u> by William Oates Ragsdale.  It is the story of Scots-Irish farmers of the Presbyterian faith from North Carolina who immigrated to Pope County, Arkansas.  They named their settlements Pisgah and Bethany based on the names from the area they had left in Gaston County, North Carolina.  Pisgah Cemetery is a large active cemetery west of the town of Pottsville, Arkansas.

**From Chapter 7 of Ragsdale's book The Pisgah Home Front in War and Reconstruction, page 87:**

*Melissa McElwee Oates, whose husband Thomas was serving in the Confederate army, was left with at least five children to feed. She buried provisions to keep the bushwhackers from finding them, but she also faced the visits of Federal troops seeking supplies.  One day, when they visited her farm, an officer found a bolt of woolen cloth which Melissa had made, took it, and tied it on his saddle.  As he was about to ride away, Melissa came up to the horse, untied the bolt, and told the officer, "I made this for clothes for my children."  Reports coming through the Wade Oates family  say that the officer did not say a word and let her keep the cloth without controversy.  Melissa's resourcefulness was reflected in other actions.  When she received word that her husband had been shot in the neck and was recuperating after the battle at Jenkins' Ferry in April 1864, she hitched an oxen team to a wagon, loaded her children, and went to Jenkins' Ferry, where she became Thomas's nurse.  She and the children stayed until he was on his way to recovery........The actions of Melissa Oates and other brave women demonstrate that survival of the community depended much upon the resourcefulness of the women.*

**From Chapter 7 page 80,  more about Melissa's family:**

*It is difficult to say that one Pisgah family suffered any more than another as a result of the war, but the agonies of some families were monumental.  In April 1863, Elizabeth Neely McElwee (1797-1863) died and was buried at Pisgah.  She and her husband William, who had been senior immigrants of the early 1850's had been touched deeply by the war. Their son William had been killed, leaving a wife and young daughter. Their son-in-law, Joseph D. Oates died in Mississippi. leaving a wife and two young boys. Daughters Melissa and Elizabeth Z. had husbands in the war. Elizabeth's husband, Dr. Alexander W. Henry, served as a doctor in the Confederate service. In 1864, he contracted malaria and died in service. The McElwees also had grandsons Thomas B. and James McElwee in service.*

It is obvious that Melissa's effort in nursing Thomas back to health was successful, as he outlived her until after the turn of the century. They are buried in Pisgah Cemetery with identical tombstones. Thomas, born January 23, 1821 died on December 15, 1904 and Melissa born February 26, 1829 died on February 8, 1900.

Original "spit and whittle" bench that sat in front of the Keener store in downtown Pottsville.  It was purchased by Mandy and Michael Keener (grandchildren of Herman and Floy) as a Father's Day gift for their dad, David Keener. *Courtesy of Beverly Keener.*

W P A bridge built in 1941 is 5 miles south of Pottsville on River Road. *Courtesy of author's collection.*

# Homes

Homes in Pottsville, like the residents were varied in style and personality.  The first homes made of logs and rock chimneys provided shelter, but very little of the comforts we enjoy today.  Imagine the pioneer settler who had to first clear the land and level a spot; then cut the trees into logs of the correct size and length to build a cabin.  All of those early log homes have disappeared today.

Images on the following pages are homes in the Pottsville area built before 1940.  Some have been beautifully restored, some are vacant and dilapidated and many are gone.   Some have been moved from one location to another and are still loved and maintained.  Others, like the Dr. Jean home is an example of a unique period of time in America when a complete house, electrical and plumbing supplies, paint and everything needed could be ordered from a mail order catalog, Sears and Roebuck.  There were other kit houses in the area, but the Ray and Sue Tucker (Dr. Jean's) home is the only one remaining.

As saw mills became available for local timber use, many houses in Pottsville were a standard white two-story house with a porch across the front and maybe a second story balcony.  Most of those were built around 1900 to accommodate large families.  It was before indoor plumbing was introduced, so building up was less expensive than building a larger home.

The first brick home was the Blake house close to the school.  Now, Pottsville has many modern brick homes and like the early settlers, homes vary in style and size.

Thomas and Melissa Oates lived in this home on Pisgah Road before the Civil War. *Author's collection.*

Known as the Falls place, this home was located just east of the end of River Road. From 1940-1952 Claude and Anna Denny family lived there and farmed. When the oxbow of the Arkansas River was straightened in 1952 to prepare for the dam to be built, much of the farm land disappeared. That made it necessary for the family to move. Son Floyd remembers playing under the dog trot porch and good memories of the house with his twin Lloyd and six siblings *Author's collection.*

Home of Dr. R.H. Gardner — Pottsville, Ark. Built in the 1880's and called "The House of Seven Gables."

*From the Pope County Arkansas History Book vol 2.*

Allmon home place on east side of River Road about 5 miles south of Pottsville

The top photograph shows the William Bell Home.



The Will Bell home was built around 1900 and was located about 3 miles south of Pottsville on Narrow Road.  At that time, Narrow Road went through cotton farm land and connected with the South New Hope community.  Shown on the front porch are Mr. Bell, wife Margaret Dickey Bell and daughters Mattie and Maggie.  *Courtesy of the Charles Oates collection.*

Mattie & Maggie Bell

The Bryson home was located directed across River Road from the Presbyterian Church. It was the home of the Reverend Clifford Bryson who served the Presbyterian Church as a long-time pastor.

In 2020, during the Covid-19 Pandemic, the home was moved to a new location on Cedar Street (also known as Dog Alley) to allow for expansion of the Pottsville Baptist Church on that property. *Author's collection.*

Alex Corbett Home, Reed's Ferry area. Front part of this home was close to the road and served as a store with a barber chair.  When Alex married and began a family, the house was moved rolling on giant logs to the current spot and back additions added.

From the files of the Atkins Chronicle July 21, 1916
*Alex Corbett is putting a ferry on the Arkansas River at the mouth of Petit Jean river.  The ferry will be so arranged that landing can be made on west bank of the Petit Jean and get traffic from Carden Bottoms and also land on the east bank and get traffic from Perry County.  The landing on the north bank of the Arkansas will be almost directly south of Atkins.*

According to the Pope County, Arkansas History Book, this ferry was located ten miles below Dardanelle in 1934.                           .
*Courtesy of the Pope County History Book.*

Sears Roebuck Company, founded in 1886 was one of the world's largest mass merchandiser  mail-order company.  While most people know that Sears Roebuck sold nearly everything for the home from its mail order catalogue, few realize that it also sold houses. Between 1908 and 1940 Sears operated a "Modern Homes" division that supplied building plans and materials Kit houses were shipped to all corners of the nation.  The package included the entire house, with numbered parts and instruction booklets, paint and nails.  There were 22 different styles ranging in price from a low price of $650.00 to the deluxe model at $2,500.00

Dr. R. M. Jean, a Pottsville physician for 28 years, ordered this home from Sears Roebuck and it was assembled in January of 1917. Located on River Road just north of the school campus, in 2011 it was moved by Ray and Sue Tucker to Hwy 64 west of Atkins. Dr. Jean's home information provided by Ray Tucker. *Author's collection.*

The Daniels' home place was built around the turn of the century and faced east toward the Parker home which faced west. Wade and Bessie Jane Daniels purchased the home from George Rodgers on October 2, 1917 and lived there for more than 58 years.

The last residents of this home were Ben and Nina Daniels Rice who completed renovated it. In 2021, this beautiful home still stands. *Author's collection.*

The Duffield home then and now located on the corner of Hwy 64 and River Road.
*Courtesy of David Duffield*

Falls' home located on River Road just south of the Presbyterian Church was owned by Roy Falls who was co-owner of the Falls-Sinclair General Mercantile store.

The hitching post was from the days when horses or buggies were the primary mode of transportation. The Falls' name is inscribed in the front sidewalk. In 2021, the house still stands. *Author's collection.*

Forrest Henry home, located across from the current Pottsville Elementary School was owned by the Pottsville druggist. In 2021, the house still stands. *Courtesy of Sue Roberts.* Below is John and Verna Stewart's home on Narrow Road. *Author's collection.*

Charles Oates in front of his grandparents, Thomas and Lizzie Oates home .
*Courtesy of the Charles Oates collection.*

Centerpiece of Parkers' plantation this large two-story home was owned by Silas Reece Parker. Construction of the Parker family home began in the 1840s. Cypress wood was hauled from a cypress brake at present day Lake Atkins. Parker operated a grist mill and general store on Galla Creek. Later the home was owned by the Robertson family and remained in their family for over a century until it was the house was torn down to make day for the new Pottsville Butterfield bypass. *Author's collection.*

John Pryor home place was located on West Ash Street, just past the Baptist Church. *Courtesy of Kenneth Taylor.*

Group in front of Verna Stewart's home located on Dog Alley (Cedar Street). *Courtesy of Kenneth Taylor.*

Rankin Home located across from the Pottsville Fire Department was built around 1900. Mrs. Rankin loved to entertain and always had a Seniors graduation party. It now sits empty.
*Author's collection.*

First brick home in Pottsville, Blake Home located on River Road close to the Elementary school. Charles Blake was a rural mail carrier and a member of the Pottsville Associate Reformed Presbyterian Church. In 2021, the house still stands. *Author's collection.*

J.A. (Ott) Motley home place located on State Hwy 331 west of Pottsville.  Seven sons, J.E. (Pat), Glenn, Robert, J.M (Connie), Jack, Jay and Ray and one daughter Ila Mae grew up in this house. *Author's collection.*

Harry and Leona Barge home, located just south of the Bethany Church on River Road.  The family moved from Minnesota in 1954 and the youngest child, Margaret Barge Motley, with her husband Allan still live on family acreage. *Author's collection.*

Gregory and Margaret Sinclair moved to Pope County in 1855. They built a two-story home about a mile east of Pottsville on the Military Road, now Hwy 64.

Son John joined the Confederate Army when he turned 18 in 1864. When the war ended in 1865, the mare he had ridden the entire time recognized that he was close to home and began to neigh, and the family was alerted that their son was home.

The large home served the family for over a century. The Sinclair barn is now on the grounds of the Potts Inn and displays agriculture items. *Courtesy of Pope County Historical Foundation*

In 1939 Boyce Sinclair built a new brick home just south of the Pottsville School grounds and it remains today. *Author's collection.*

Located on Combs Road, off of Pine Ridge Road was the Teeter home, which was later purchased by Albert "Buttermilk" Davis. *Courtesy of Kenneth Taylor.*

The remains of the Harold Stewart home located on Narrow Road. At one time Narrow Road ran in front of this house, now it runs in the back.  Large cotton fields stretched out in front of this house. *Author's collection.*

The Will Kessler place was located 3 miles south of Pottsville on the east side of River Road.  It was later the Frank Wheeler place and still remains today.  *Courtesy of Charles Oates collection.*

Dr. Whiteside's home located approximately a mile south of Pottsville on River Road.  The Teeter family later purchased the home.  In 2021, the house still stands. *Courtesy of  Kenneth Taylor*

The old Morton home place located on the Old Military Road west of Pottsville was built in 1885. The first residents were Rueben Oliver, his wife Madred and their children Thomas H., Louis Allen, Hugh Dudley, Lorenzo Dow and Lillie Bell. Peddlers frequently stopped for a noon meal and sometimes for lodging. Even many years after the Civil War, in the 1890's Union-Southern soldiers travelers arguments were still common. The Morton's only daughter, Lillie married Will Rankin, owner of the Pottsville cotton gin.

In the 1950's & 1960s, the property was owned by Dr. J.N. Thompson, his wife June and two sons. Dr. Thompson was a founding pioneer in the poultry industry in Arkansas.

Shown in the photo are Chuck and Janie Frankhouse who owned the house in 1997 and opened the home for a tour as a part of the Pottsville Centennial celebration. In 2021, the house still stands. *Author's collection.*

The oldest existing home in Pottsville is Potts Inn completed in 1858. *Author's collection.*

# Pope County Historical Foundation

In 1968, Marge Crabaugh became interested in saving and restoring Potts Inn.  Already an active citizen, Mrs. Crabaugh used her connections within the community to rally support for the project.  The Pope County Historical Foundation was formed.  The Foundation met the challenge of preserving the Inn, and it's history.  Without Marge's dedication to preserving this home, it probably wouldn't exist today.

Potts Inn was listed on the National Register of Historic Places in 1970 and purchased that same year.  Owned by the county but overseen by a board of Directors, the next few years were filled with fundraising and restoration activities.  The Inn was finally ready to open regularly as a museum for tours in the summer of 1975.

Marge Crabaugh served as the president of the Foundation's Board of Directors for the first two decades of its existence.  She worked tirelessly to promote and preserve the Potts Inn. Marge was followed by David Vance and later, Charles Oates, both well versed in the history of the area.  Taking over as President of the Board following Charles Oates, Pam Scarber served the Potts Inn securing grant money for improvements.  Margaret Motley is the current Board President.

It has been over fifty years since the house was purchased and restored.  Many Board members have given generously of their time to continue to maintain and improve the museum making preservation truly a group effort.  The Pope County Quorum Court oversees the budget to pay for utilities, day to day expenses, and the tour guide.  The City of Pottsville has generously helped maintain the grounds.  The Pottsville Police Department watches the Inn from across the street and contacts Board members and employees  if anything unusual occurs.  The Pottsville Masons have donated for specific projects regularly. The Pottsville School district is supportive.  Each year students are encouraged to participate in the Founders' Day activities.   Visitors are delighted to see school kids dressed in period costumes illustrating daily life of the Pioneers.  It is through the cooperation, dedication, and care of so many that Potts Inn continues to welcome travelers to the River Valley.

This photo of the Potts family home shows the condition of the Inn before restoration in 1970. Mary Potts, daughter of James and Ada Potts and third generation Potts family member was the last descendant to live in the Inn. Mary never married and events at the Potts home were of the greatest joy to her.

The house had been divided in half during the mid 1900's. Sharing the home with Mary was Faye Potts, widow of John Potts, (great, grandson of Kirkbride and Pamelia) who lived on the east side (which was closest to the street.) Faye was a teacher in the Pottsville School District and loved to have students come and visit.

The lengthy and complicated process of acquisition of Potts Inn home by Pope County was headed by Marge Crabaugh. Also involved were Mary Hall (great, granddaughter of Kirkbride and Pamelia Potts), other Potts family members, and the Pope County Historical Foundation Board of Directors. The home's importance, not only as a local social and cultural center, but the three years as a stagecoach stop for Butterfields's Overland Mail Company was understood by this group. A huge debt is owed to this amazing woman, Marge Crabaugh. *Courtesy of the Pope County Historical Foundation.*

Potts Inn before restoration. *Courtesy of the Pope County Historical Foundation.*

Potts family smokehouse before restoration was begun. *Courtesy of the Pope County Historical Foundation.*

Painting of Marge Craubaugh that hangs in the Ladies Parlor of the Potts Inn. *Courtesy of the Pope County Historical Foundation.*

1970 Board of Directors of the Pope County Historical Foundation. Marge Crabaugh, J.C. Jones, Toni Weatherford, David Vance, Rebecca Stowers and Mr. Morrisey, . *Courtesy of the Pope County Historical Foundation.*

A time capsule was buried on the lawn of Potts Inn as a part of the 1997 Centennial celebration.  The 1997 Pottsville Centennial was such a huge success, Butterfield Days became a annual event. *Courtesy of the Pope County Historical Foundation.*

# Pottsville Today

Pottsville  (72858) is located in the southern portion of Pope County.  The County seat of Russellville is located in a broad valley six miles to the west of Pottsville.  Pope County is bordered on the north by the Ozark Mountains and on the south by the Ouachita Mountains with the Arkansas River flowing through the valley.  It is easy to understand why Kirkbride Potts chose this location for his new home in 1828.  North of his home was the beautiful Crow Mountain (sometimes old maps refer to it as Carrion Crow Mountain) and the Military Road carried that carried travelers across the Arkansas Territory.  Today U.S.  Highway 64 has replaced the Military Road and Interstate 40, one of the busiest Interstates in the nation provides the transportation for thousands of vehicles every day; right past the first Potts home place.

Kirkbride Potts could have never imaged the community that was named in his honor .  Even a visionary like Potts could not have imagined the changes 163 years would bring to the world and to Pottsville.  The reader who visit this area will see the vision of the Founders in the excellent School District, several active churches, a recently dedicated new City Hall, a professional Police and Fire Department.   Kirkbride might also have been amazed at the transformation of leisure time, these centuries later.   Modern Pottsville citizens still value Kirkbride's passion for books, and reading by the fire.   Citizens of his namesake,  Pottsville, have continued his value of family, health, team work as they gather at our local parks.   Rev. Morris Athletic Complex is always busy with competitive softball and baseball games and a walking trail.  Rankin Park has playground equipment, picnic tables and public restrooms.   Families and friends gather at these parks, to continue the Pioneer spirit of family and community.  The visitor will meet its citizens, people that care about each other and the rich history that is ours to treasure.

The population sign in July of 2021 will soon be updated to the new numbers from the recent census. The town has grown in the ten years since the last census and it is estimated the new number will be approximately 3,500. Retail businesses in Pottsville in 2021 are: Arkansas River Pizza, Centennial Bank, Cypress Valley Meats, Gary's Sharpening, Pottsville Pharmacy, Fletcher Convenience store, Powell Boots, Tammy Lou's Cafe, Fleet Tire, Galla Creek Golf Course, Potts Inn Museum, Terminix, Dollar General, Bruckner Truck, The Nail Room, Junkin Paradise, and C & C Towing and Recovery and Pottsville Car Wash  *Author's collection.*

Pottsville Mayor and City Council members:  From left, Kevin Burnham, Randall Blalock, Steve Williamson, City Attorney Deidre Luker, Mayor Randy Tankersley, City Recorder Holly Fowler, John Heflin and Clint Maness.  Absent George Woolf.
*Author's collection.*

Pottsville School Board:  From left to right, David Potts, Jim Huffman, Tracy Taylor, Clint Hull and Jeff Akin.  *Courtesy of Larry Dugger, Superintendent of the Pottsville School District.*

Pottsville Masons:  L to R:  Bill Teeter, Senior Warden, Vernon Lawhorn, Tyler, Tracy Thurman, Junior Warden, R. W. Eric Westcott, Senior Deacon, Randy Tankersley, Junior Master of Ceremony, Hayden Darr, Senior Master of Ceremony, Tiger Westcott, Junior Deacon.  *Author's collection.*

Pottsville Police Department. *Author's collection.*

Logo on Pottsville Officer's badges. *Courtesy of the Pottsville Police Chief Joe Paterak.*

Pottsville Fire Department. *Author's collection.*

Pottsville Fire Department members pose in front of a controlled burn conducted at the former home of Jewel Rodden. It was burned to make room for the Baptist Church expansion. *Courtesy of Pottsville Fire Chief Brad Jenkins.*

United States Post Office.  Pottsville's current Postmaster is Valerie Allman.  *Author's collection.*

Commemorative stamp designed for the annual Butterfield Days celebration.  *Courtesy of Pope County Historical Foundation.*

Photo taken August 28, 2020 during Senator Boozman's visit to the Potts Inn.

Pope County Historical Foundation Board members (L to R) Carl Kirkley, Tonya Oates, David Oates, Cathy Baker, Arkansas Department of Parks, Heritage, and Tourism Secretary Stacy Hurst, Garry Penman, Margaret Motley, museum tour guide Kara Bowers, the Honorable Senator John Boozman (R-AR), Arkansas Tourism Director Travis Napper, Jarrod Toland, Pope County Library Director Sherry Simpson

Board members not pictured:  Sue Roberts, Tina Taylor, Sadra Hill, Riley Taurone, George Woolf, David and Sandy Vance.

*. Courtesy of Arkansas Senator John Boozman.*

*Author's collection.*

Inside the Rev. Morris Athletic Complex are three softball fields named in honor of Jerry Day, Jerry Duvall, and Clint Hall. Also, a little league field named in honor of Kenneth Taylor, and a baseball field named in honor of George Woolf. There is also a walking trail named to honor Adolf Vodrazka. Known as Mr. Vod, he was a popular Agri teacher for many years. *Author's collection.*

Pope County Judge Ben Cross, Payroll Deputy Elaine Thompson, and Administrative Assistant to Judge Cross, Laura McGuire. The Potts Inn is owned by Pope County and we sincerely appreciate their support. *Author's collection.*

Authors Margaret Motley. and Kara Bowers *Author's collection.*

February 2021 Potts Inn with snow. *Author's collection.*